NASA SP-2003-4530

The Spoken Word: Recollections of Dryden History, The Early Years

edited by
Curtis Peebles

NASA History Division
Office of Policy and Plans
NASA Headquarters
Washington, DC 20546

Monographs in
Aerospace History
Number 30
2003

Library of Congress Cataloging-in-Publication Data

The spoken word : recollections of Dryden history : the early years / Curtis L. Peebles, editor.
    p. cm. -- (Monographs in aerospace history ; no. 30)
  Includes bibliographical references and indes.
  1. NASA Dryden Flight Research Center--History. 2. Aeronautics--Reserach--California--Rogers Lake (Kern County)--History. 3. Aeronautical engineers--United States--Interviews. 4. Airplanes--United States--Flight testing. 5. Oral history. I. Peebles, Curtis. II. Series.

TL568.N23U62003
629.13'007'2079488–dc21

                                                2002045204

For sale by the U.S. Government Printing Office
Superintendent of Documents, Mail Stop: SSOP, Washington, DC 20402-9328

Table of Contents

Section I: Foundations 1

    Walter C. Williams 7

    Clyde Bailey, Richard Cox, Don Borchers, and Ralph Sparks 19

    John Griffith 47

    Betty Love 55

Section II: A Second Wind 63

    Richard E. Day 67

    Scott Crossfield 77

    Jack Fischel 87

    Stanley P. Butchart 101

Epilogue 125

Sources 126

About the Author 127

Acknowledgments 127

Index 128

The NASA History Series 130

Front Cover: Ma Greene's Cafe, Muroc, California
Back Cover: Scott Crossfield, the D-558-II, P2B, F-86 chase planes and support personnel.
Book design by Steve Lighthill, NASA Dryden Flight Research Center.
All photos of individuals are in the Dryden photo archives

Editor's Forward

Since the founding of the Dryden Flight Research Center History Office in 1996, its staff has conducted nearly a hundred interviews with retired and serving employees. Their recollections represent a unique resource in understanding the development of aerospace technology in the second half of the 20th century. Their personal experiences, insights, and opinions allow the reader to gain an understanding into what it was actually like to have been involved with some of the milestone events in aerospace history. These interviews have been edited and assembled into this monograph, so that a wider audience can also share in their experiences.

This study covers the early years of what eventually became the Dryden Flight Research Center. It spans the period between the arrival of Walter Williams and the first group of NACA engineers at Muroc in 1946, and ends with the establishment of NASA in 1958. This timeframe encompasses the breaking of the sound barrier, the pivotal inertial coupling research, the first use of computer simulations, the transformation of the NACA facility from an old hangar into a state-of-the-art research center, and the dawn of the space age. These events took place against the background of the end of World War II, the start of the Cold War, and the twin technological revolutions of jet propulsion and supersonic flight. They are told by the people who participated in these events, in their own words.

Curtis Peebles
January 2003

Section I

Foundations

The foundations of the Dryden Flight Research Center date back more than a half century, to a time when aviation faced revolutionary technical changes. When the first NACA contingent arrived in September 1946, they found the Muroc Army Air Field to be an isolated and barren outpost. The post-war demobilization had left the hastily constructed base facilities in a poor state of repair. Palmdale and Lancaster in the late 1940s were rough desert towns lacking many of the conveniences to which the new arrivals from Langley (and their spouses) had been accustomed. Farther north lay Mojave, a desolate railroad stop with a gas station, White's Motel, a nightclub, and a pool hall. Rosamond consisted of little more than several bars open around the clock. Agriculture continued to be the primary activity in the Antelope Valley: cattle and grain on the west side, and alfalfa farming on the east.

The high desert was not the only roughhewn part of Southern California. Los Angeles—still a long drive from the Antelope Valley on a two-lane, winding mountain road—remained a hard-boiled city, despite its rapidly growing population and sophistication. Kevin Starr, the State Librarian of California described this booming metropolis at the time of the first X-1 flights:

> "It was a Front Page kind of city, the Los Angeles of 1947: a city of cops, crooks, and defense lawyers; a demimonde of rackets, screaming headlines, and politicians on the take; a town of gamblers, guys and dolls, booze and sex; a place for schemers, also-rans, suckers and those who deceived them: the kind of city in which a private detective such as Philip Marlowe might make his way down mean streets in search of the ever-elusive truth and get sapped with a blackjack for his efforts by parties unknown."

The Muroc train station circa 1940, shortly before the Army facility on the lakebed was expanded to serve as a training base. (Air Force photo)

In contrast to the evolving young city to the south, the landscape around Muroc was an ancient one. Large dry lakebeds — scattered across the desert from southern California to eastern Nevada — were remnants of cooler, wetter times at the end of the last ice age. The largest of these, Rogers Dry Lake, covers some 47.3 square miles of the Mojave desert. During each brief winter, rains carried silt onto the Rogers lakebed, and the winds blew the mixture of water and sediment across its surface. With the arrival of each spring, the high temperatures dried out and hardened the now-smooth lakebed. The process, repeated each year, occurred over the millennia.

The first permanent settlers in the vicinity of Rogers Dry Lake were Clifford and Effie Corum, their two children, and Clifford's brother Ralph, who arrived at the site in 1910. They settled on a homestead on the west side of the lakebed, and were soon joined by a few other hardy souls. The small farming community–named "Muroc" (Corum spelled backwards)–consisted of a one-room school house, a general store, and scattered homes. It also served as a watering stop on the Atchison Topeka & Santa Fe Railway. For the next two decades, Muroc remained a tiny cluster of buildings in the midst of the desert.

In September 1933, destiny caught up with Muroc, when a U.S. Army Air Corps detachment from March Field arrived to set up the Muroc Bombing and Gunnery Range on the east side of the lakebed. For the next decade, March Field squadrons undertook training activities and war games, while a small group of noncommissioned officers and enlisted men at East Camp, on the opposite side of the lakebed from Muroc, maintained the targets. They lived in tents and slept on mattresses stuffed with straw. During the exercises, Army Air Corps squadrons landed their aircraft on the lakebed, and the crews also lived in tents during the week or so they underwent training. A second camp was established on the west side of the lakebed in 1934. Muroc's role expanded in July 1941 with the arrival by train of 140 troops, who set up a tent camp on the southwest edge of the Rogers lakebed. They began construction of a training field, later called Muroc Army Air Field, to meet the increased need for pilots following the outbreak of the war in Europe.

West of Rogers, another part of the area developed. In March 1935, Pasadena socialite and aviatrix Florence "Pancho" Barnes bought an alfalfa farm close to the shore of Rosamond Dry Lake. Pancho soon worked out an arrangement to supply the Muroc personnel with fresh milk and pork. As the base expanded in the 1940s, she added a roadhouse restaurant and bar catering to the pilots and officers. Within a few years, this had grown into a 368-acre dude ranch called the Rancho Oro Verde. More commonly called the "Happy Bottom Riding Club," it included a motel, dance hall, swimming pool, horse corral and barns, an airstrip with hangars and a tower, and a reputation that became legendary.

The sudden U.S. entry into World War II in December 1941 saw an acceleration of the construction at Muroc. An all-weather concrete runway, hangars, a tower, and a parking apron all materialized. The headquarters building, base hospital, and other structures were described as "marvels of tarpaper, wire, and wood." During this period, Muroc served as an advanced training base, where P-38 fighter pilots and B-24 and B-25 bomber crews received their final instructions before being sent overseas. They took some of their bombing practice on the "Muroc Maru," a timber and chicken wire silhouette of a full-sized Japanese Atago-class heavy cruiser. To accommodate the mass influx of people to the desert, a tent city sprang up to house the new arrivals near Muroc. Also nearby, "Kerosene Flats" became the housing area for married personnel. At the other end of the lakebed, at Muroc Flight Test Base, flight tests began on the Bell XP-59A Airacomet, the first U.S.-built jet aircraft. Because the vicinity of Wright Field, Ohio, was too populated for the classified Airacomet to remain secret, in April 1942, Muroc became the XP-59A's test site. A hangar, barracks, and water tower rose from the sand, and on October 1, 1942, the aircraft made its initial flights, ushering the

The Muroc Maru was a full-scale replica of a Japanese cruiser used for bombing practice. Officially called Temporary Building T-799, the lumber and chicken wire structure cost $35,819.18 to build. The decaying hulk remained on the south end of the lakebed after the war, until finally being demolished on February 13, 1950. (Air Force photo)

U.S. into the jet age. The XP-59A also shaped the future of Muroc. To the project officers and engineers working on the Airacomet, the advantages of Muroc over Wright Field — year-round clear weather, open spaces, and proximity to the Los Angeles aircraft industries — became obvious.

In late 1943 and early 1944, the Army Air Forces leadership considered a proposal to convert all of the Muroc facilities into a flight test center. Although rejected at the time due to the importance of Muroc's training activities, Army Air Forces leaders decided that Muroc would be converted to test work once the war was over. Consequently, after 1945, the facilities at Muroc Army Air Field, (now called South Base) and the expanded Muroc Flight Test Base, (now North Base), served as the initial test sites. The Army Air Forces also committed itself to a Master Plan for a new, modernized base along the western shore of the lakebed, near Muroc.

The need for a new flight test facility had become inescapable. The higher performance aircraft developed during the war entered uncharted speed regimes. Pilots found that as they made high speed dives, their aircraft shook and the controls became ineffective. Aerodynamicists knew these phenomena involved the increase in drag and the formation of shockwaves as aircraft approached transonic flight. Even before the Wright brothers, wind tunnels had been used to understand aerodynamic forces. But in this new situation, they could provide no help. At velocities from just below the speed of sound to just above, data from existing wind tunnels became unreliable.

In light of these obstacles, researchers such as John Stack at the Langley Memorial Aeronautical Laboratory in Hampton, Virginia decided that only one way existed to continue the exploration of transonic flight: build specialized research aircraft, instrument them thoroughly, and fly them near and above Mach 1. Even before World War II ended, two such aircraft began development. The Navy funded the Douglas D-558-I Skystreak. The designers of the jet-powered Skystreak intended it to reach speeds close to Mach 1. The Army Air Forces backed a far different Mach 1 contender. The Bell X-1 was powered by a rocket engine, a form of propulsion that engineers in the mid-1940s viewed as suspect. It was carried aloft by a B-29, then fell away from the mothership, and the pilot ignited the rockets. The X-1 was designed not just to approach the speed of sound, but to exceed it. Although very different in purpose, these two aircraft actually complemented each other. The X-1 had the higher top speed, but could sustain it for only a brief time before its rocket engine consumed all of its fuel. The D-558-I, in contrast, flew slower, but could sustain a cruise speed above Mach 0.8 for a half hour at a time.

Both the Army and the Navy asked the National Advisory Committee for Aeronautics (NACA) to equip the X-1 and D-558-I with instrumentation, assist with flight planning, and analyze the data at the end of the flights. Once the initial contractor and military test program had finished, the aircraft would be transferred to the NACA for its own research activities. To support the X-1 flights, a small team from Langley, led by a young but experienced engineer named Walter C. Williams, was organized. The initial NACA involvement began with the X-1 glide flights at Pinecastle Field, Florida between January and March of 1946. That summer, Langley dispatched the NACA support team to Muroc. The first two engineers, George P. Minalga and Harold B. Youngblood, arrived on September 15, 1946. Williams reached Muroc on September 30. He was joined the same day by Cloyce E. Matheny, and William S. Aiken came soon after. This initial group of five engineers became known as the NACA Muroc Flight Test Unit. Another group of six engineers and technicians arrived at Muroc on October 9. In December, two "computers," Roxanah Yancey and Isabell Martin, arrived at Muroc. The term then referred to technicians-mostly women-who performed the laborious math calculations needed to reduce the instrument readings into engineering data.

As the new arrivals adjusted to their surroundings, they found themselves in a place far from the green landscape of Hampton Virginia, with few of the refinements to which they were accustomed. But none of that mattered. As the year 1947 began, they had other things on their minds. At this place, and in this sky, they flew an airplane faster than any had ever flown before; faster, indeed, than some thought possible.

NACA research aircraft at the original South Base hangar. From left to right are the D-558-II Skyrocket, D-558-I Skystreak, X-5, X-1#2, X-4, and the delta wing XF-92A. (E-145)

The initial NACA group at Muroc slowly expanded as the X-1 flights began in the spring of 1947. The Muroc Flight Test Unit occupied a hangar at South Base, next to one used by Douglas Aircraft. Resources were few, the work was demanding, the base commander offered minimal support, and management at Langley was far away. The team learned to improvise, and to do their tasks quickly, with a minimum of paperwork and deliberations.

On October 14, 1947, about a year after the first NACA engineers arrived in the desert, Capt. Chuck Yeager made the first Mach 1 flight. Soon, operational F-86 jet fighters exceeded Mach 1 in dives. Even so, the X-1 represented only the first step. The new frontier of supersonic flight held many unknowns. The demands it presented meant that virtually every aspect of aircraft technology had to change. Structures, airfoils, control systems, fuel systems, life support, escape systems, weapons, electronics, and propulsion all had to meet the demands of speeds and altitudes far in excess of those reached only a few years before. Entirely new wing shapes-swept wings and delta wings, both with and without horizontal stabilizers, as well as variable-sweep wings, and low-aspect ratio straight wings-were proposed to deal with these unknowns.

In addition to the revolution in aviation technology, another factor animated the research programs: the emerging Cold War with the Soviet Union. To cope with the threat posed by the Soviet bloc, faster and more capable aircraft had to be developed on an accelerated basis. With aviation technology rapidly changing, new designs surpassed aircraft that had first flown only a short time before. As a consequence, the Air Force pressed to get data quickly, in order to design the next generation of combat aircraft. The NACA, in contrast, remained committed to patient, step-by-step research programs. This approach remained consistent with its long tradition of discovering the underlying principals that governed flight.

To push the limits of flight to higher speeds and altitudes, new experimental aircraft were developed. The Air Force funded research on an advanced series of X-1 aircraft, able to reach speeds above Mach 2. Bell Aircraft designed and fabricated the X-2, an advanced rocket aircraft with swept wings, and able to reach Mach 3. The Navy also investigated swept wings, with the Douglas D-558-II. This design differed completely from both the D-558-I or the X-2. The D-558-II did have swept wings, but also, initially, both a rocket engine and a jet engine.

At the same time, a number of new wing configurations appeared on supersonic aircraft, as well as on other X-planes. Low-aspect ratio wings flew on the Douglas X-3, while a tailless swept wing design flew on the Northrop X-4. The Bell X-5 took a different approach. On this aircraft, the wings pivoted, so their sweep angle could be changed in flight. The wings extended at take off (to give maximum lift), and could be swept back at high speeds (to reduce drag). An unsuccessful fighter prototype, the Convair XF-92A, tested a delta wing design. Consistent with the earlier research aircraft, the NACA participated in the contractor and military tests, then used the X-planes for its own flight research programs.

These new X-planes and the demands of a rapidly evolving aviation technology finally transformed Muroc into a modern military base. The Air Force became an independent service in September 1947, and redesignated the facility Muroc Air Force Base (AFB). Meantime, the hurriedly constructed wartime buildings deteriorated during the post-war years, and by 1949 their condition had become poor. The first step toward renovation involved the construction of pre-fabricated concrete housing for base personnel. On January 27, 1950, Muroc was renamed Edwards; in honor of Capt. Glen Edwards, killed in the crash of a prototype YB-49A flying wing. The following year, the Air Force Flight Test Center opened at Edwards AFB, with responsibility for aircraft tests, the operation of test facilities, and for support of contractors and other government agencies (such as the NACA).

Meanwhile a new test facility (called "Main Base"), rose between the old North and South Base, located near the original Muroc settlement, Kerosene Flats, and the wartime tent camp. Construction crews razed the old buildings, built a new, longer runway, and added a new tower, taxiways and hangars. By 1954, Pancho's had been bought out and, with the addition of Rosamond Dry Lake, the size of the base nearly doubled. The railroad tracks which had crossed Rogers Dry Lake were removed, allowing its full surface to be used for landings and takeoffs. "Contractor's Row," the facilities used by the aircraft and engine companies, went up along the shoreline to the north of Main Base. Transfer of test activities to Main Base occurred gradually; flight testing continued at North Base into 1954, the base headquarters did not move from South Base until August 1955, and the Air Force Test Pilot School finally left South Base in March of 1956.

As the Master Plan became a reality, the NACA group underwent its own changes in terms of structure and living conditions. At the time of Yeager's flight, the NACA Muroc Flight Test Unit employed 27 individuals. A little over a year later, in January 1948, the number more than doubled to 60 people. By January 1950, the workforce doubled again, growing to 132 personnel. Just as Muroc became Edwards AFB, the NACA Flight Test Unit became the NACA High-Speed Flight Research Station.

With the construction of Main Base, the NACA personnel left their cramped, makeshift quarters at South Base. With the growing size and importance of the station, a decision was reached to build a fully capable research center in the desert. In August 1951, Congress appropriated a total of $4 million for its construction. The Air Force leased to the NACA a section of the shoreline north of Contractor's Row. Shovels broke ground on January 27, 1953, and construction began the following month. The NACA facility consisted of a main building with a hangar on either side, a parking apron and taxiway, and shop buildings. The new facility opened formally on June 26, 1954. On July 1, 1954, it was re-named the High-Speed Flight Station. These buildings, much expanded and remodeled, still form the core of the Dryden Flight Research Center a half century later.

WALTER C. WILLIAMS

Interview by John Terreo, August 6, 1993

Walter C. Williams was the father of what is now the Dryden Flight Research Center. Energetic and demanding, he bridged the era from subsonic propeller aircraft to the dawn of hypersonics and spaceflight. Williams led the first group of personnel to arrive at Muroc in September 1946, oversaw the NACA involvement in the X-1 test flights, the expansion of the NACA team in the late 1940s and early 1950s, presided over the move from South Base, and directed the High-Speed Flight Station through the creation of NASA and the initial X-15 flights. Williams left in September 1959 to become the Associate Director of the NASA Space Task Group, and later the Director of Operations for Project Mercury.

Q: Mr. Williams, could we start out with a little background on the circumstances that brought you to Edwards? As I understand it, it was the X-1 project.

A: It was the X-1 project. I had been the NACA Flight Project Engineer, almost from the creation of the program. In other words, I was in charge of the NACA tests of the X-1. I had been following it for some time before it was completed. I made several trips to Buffalo and we were laying out the plans for testing. As you know, the airplane was originally flown as a glider at Pinecastle Army Air Field in Florida, which is now Orlando International Airport. We made 10 flights there. Testing was conducted in Florida because [the lakebed at] Muroc was wet. Pinecastle was one of the few places with 10,000 feet of runway. This was to test out the air launch technique since it had not been done before. The airplane was very light. As I recall, 3,700 pounds with no tankage and no engines in the innards. We were at least a year late while we were getting ready to fly. I went to Florida. The recommendation had been made by people through the pilot that any further testing, as it got heavier with the engine, be done at Muroc. When the X-1 came to Muroc, that's when the small NACA team came to Muroc.

Q: What were the reasons for bringing the X-1 to Muroc?

A: The lake. It gave you a chance to land. See, you were landing without power and flew with no navigation. We lacked the availability of many-mile long runways. We could land in almost any direction. As it worked out, the flight planning was such that they landed on the mock runways on the lake. Until you knew a few of these things, and also filled them in with some caution, you wanted the lake.

Q: You came out here, I believe in September, 1946. Could you describe what the base was like and what the surrounding area was like, because even by today's standards, this area is remote so I imagine it must have been even more so than [today].

A: I wouldn't call it remote now at all after having driven up this morning. The base, itself, had a few temporary hangars on the North Base where the XP-59A was being tested. As I recall, North American still had it for the F-86 tests. At South Base, there was an 8,000 foot runway, two large hangars and several small hangars. The Army Air Forces, by then and this was the fall of '46, had moved most of the test work down to the South Base. Airplanes that were here were things like the XB-35, which was propeller driven, the XB-43, which was the jet version of the Douglas Mixmaster, the FJ-1, which was a North American [Aviation] jet fighter for the Navy. If it wasn't there, it was arriving soon, the Ryan FR-1 which was a combination jet and reciprocating engine airplane. Pretty soon, everything was showing up here to test because it was the best place in the world. Even though they had a good runway, you always had the lake available for emergencies. The Hughes XF-11, the reconnaissance airplane that looked like a big P-38, was tested here. It was the same airplane that he [Howard Hughes] had used. In the number one airplane, he was almost killed in a crash in Beverly Hills, I think. It was getting to be a very active place. In addition to the airplanes that were really based here for testing, other airplanes moved in for special tests such as over-weight testing, braking tests, aborted take-offs, things that you needed some extra space. The weather was very good, too.

Q: I believe that when NACA first moved out here in the [1940's], there was a little bit of reluctance on the part of the Base Commander to have you out here.

A: No, not that so much. It wasn't a question of being reluctant, he wanted to make it clear that he was in charge. They assigned us two group offices in one of the smaller hangars down on the South Base. They co-operated as best as they could within the limits. This was Colonel [Signa] Gilkey. His ambition was to build a new test base. He had what he called the Master Plan which is not [too] different from the way the Base looks now with the long runway facing the prevailing winds and so forth. He had tried to justify building the [new] base but it had not been successful. His attitude was he didn't want to have anything improved in a way that we could get by. This was for barracks, offices, hangars and everything. He would rather have them fall apart, then he could justify building a new base by the fact that there was nothing there. These were the things that we had a little problem with. We wanted to modify some barracks for

Aerial view of the High-Speed Flight Research Station at South Base in 1951. A small facility, it included only a single hangar with offices along its side, a separate office building, and a parking ramp. Among the airplanes on the ramp are a B-29 drop plane, and a D-558-II. Both the NACA and the Douglas hangars (foreground, NACA on the right) still exist. The other buildings have been torn down. (E-503)

better living for both our single males and single females. We wanted to take one of the Butler [buildings], and add some lean-tos and that would provide us with better office space, better shop space and Colonel Gilkey wouldn't have any part of that. In fact, finally we had to work through the committee of NACA which had the Chief of the Air Force, the Chief of Navy Bureau of Aeronautics and people like that. They brought the pressure on which allowed us to go ahead and make these modifications. This all came somewhat later, in 1947 and 1948.

Q: When you first came out here, and you're describing all these other projects that were coming in here, too. I suppose that housing was at a premium.

A: Housing was impossible. Most of these people who were contractors from the Los Angeles area commuted. They would fly up. They would come up and stay in the VOQ [Visiting Officer Quarters] for a week and went home on the weekends. Nobody at the time was trying to live up here if they lived in the Los Angeles area. We were not in that position. Housing wasn't very available. You could rent a motel room but that's no way to live, particularly with a family. There was Kerosene Flats which was some wartime housing right at Muroc. This was certainly sub-standard and it was full. There was a long waiting list to get into the place. You could find places here and there. I found a place to live in Palmdale which was 40 miles from the base and expensive by the standards of the time. In fact, the [Marines] had some good housing at Mojave. What they did, when the base [at Mojave] was closed down in December 1946, was to keep the housing open for their contractors and NACA people. That really opened it up for us. We could bring more people in and do some work.

Q: I've heard that trying to find temporary housing for your people was indirectly or directly related to the first time that you met Pancho. Is that true?

A: Yes, that is true. In looking around for places, I think it was Colonel [Richard R.] Shoop who said, "You might look over at Pancho's. She has a motel over there." I went over and she had a fairly nice motel for the times. She wasn't very enthusiastic about having families around. She said, "It would spoil the atmosphere. People come here to

The Kerosene Flats housing in the mid-1940s. Hurriedly built during the war as housing for married military personnel at Muroc, these wooden duplexes also served the NACA personnel who began to arrive in 1946. The site got its name from the penetrating smell of kerosene used in the heaters. Those who lived there recalled the wind and dust that penetrated the thin walls. Both Kerosene Flats and Muroc fell to construction equipment during the building of Main Base. (Air Force photo)

raise hell." It was expensive, again, by the standards of the time if you were paying motel rates not housing rents. Other than people staying there for a couple of days or something like that, I think basically we didn't use her place.

Q: The first time you met Pancho, do you have any recollection of that?

A: Yes, Pancho was Pancho, you know. I don't recall what she was doing at the time, but she was cordial and spent time with us. She started telling us about who she was and so on. She didn't think much of Gilkey as I recall.

Q: Gilkey's successor, Colonel [Albert] Boyd, I understand that he and Pancho were close.

A: They were very good friends. They got along very well. There was a different personality. Boyd was an old pilot. I should say, "Older pilot." Gilkey was an old pilot.

Q: I'd like to go back to what you were saying when you talked to Pancho about the possibility of temporary housing for some of your people and she said that she didn't want families around because the place was where you came to blow off steam. Did you visit there often?

A: Not a lot, often enough. I had my family out here and we had our life. We went to parties there.

Q: I heard that Pancho used to have parties for milestone flights.

A: Yes, we would go to those. First flights. Pancho provided the facility and the parties were usually paid for by the contractors.

Q: I have also heard that when Yeager broke the sound barrier [on October 14, 1947], NACA and some military personnel wanted to have a party out there and that was squelched because people of higher authority wanted to keep it quiet.

A: You see, a funny thing had happened there. Until we flew Mach 1, the classification of the program was classified as "Restricted," which meant that you didn't send it directly to the newspaper. Within two hours after it happened, the program was reclassified Top Secret. I got a call from the director of the NACA [Hugh L. Dryden] and he told me that. The Air Force had heard the same thing. That squelched things quite a bit.

Q: Going on the note of the sound barrier, it was a military pilot, Chuck Yeager, who flew the X-1 when it broke the sound barrier. I've heard that there was quite a bit of thinking and decision making as to whether it should be a military pilot or a contractor pilot.

A: There was discussion, but, primarily, let's start with what the agreements had been. One, that the contractor would demonstrate the airplane within known flight envelopes, like up to 0.8 Mach numbers and a few things like that. Then it was to be turned over to NACA for testing. Meanwhile, Bell managed this part of it. People thought we would piddle around too long and they wanted to charge to Mach 1 real quick. They had a proposal which included [Bell test pilot Chalmers "Slick"] Goodlin and a fairly substantial bonus. Colonel Boyd believed that nobody should be doing testing except for his flight test group and that the contractors shouldn't be doing the testing. He was a little ambivalent about NACA. Later that changed again. He and I became very good friends. He [Colonel Boyd] said, "Don't pay that guy a lot of money. We will do it. We will do an accelerated program." That's the way it happened. It was agreed that the Air Force would take on the accelerated program and we would take on the details and research program. We would also have technical surveillance of the Air Force team. They had a hell-bent-for-leather attitude. We didn't want to waste any of those pretty airplanes. (laughter) We worked day by day with the Air Force crew. We reached agreement on what would be done on the next flight. I guess, technically, we were the responsible party.

Q: To use your phrase the hell-bent-for-leather attitude, it sounds like a lot of pilots had this attitude and Pancho welcomed that kind of attitude.

A: People hadn't really learned yet and we were learning at the time by a systematic testing. Point it to the firewall and go! To go backwards to the P-47. It had dive problems. It would tuck under and you couldn't pull it out. There were three or four Army Air Forces pilots that had experienced that at Wright Field. They kept messing around with it and then one of them was killed. I, for one, thought we could do this testing without killing people by knowing what you were doing, planning ahead, taking it a bit at a time and trying to extrapolate the data which you had. That's what we did. It took us [nine] flights to get to Mach 1.

Q: Would you say that the concept of taking a little bit at a time as you evaluated and analyzed the data was really leading to a transition in flight testing?

A: Yes, it made flight test more technical.

Q: It seems like in many ways that Pancho was representative of the earlier technology.

A: I'm going to say yes and no. She was, but at the same time she had a feel for slowly walking into things instead of running.

Q: That's kind of an unusual statement regarding Pancho.

A: Once you found her out, she would run like hell.

Q: You're saying that she was cautious until she had the course spotted.

A: Yes.

Q: When you were around her, what were some of the things that she discussed. I assume airplanes.

A: Airplanes and people. I'm going to be honest. I never had a lot of conversations with Pancho because I wasn't one of those people who was there every night.

Q: You were mentioning that the contractors used to have parties there. Were these usually celebrations?

A: For first flight of a new airplane. They were all milestone flights.

Q: I've heard, too, that sometimes going away parties or promotion parties were celebrated there.

A view of the Happy Bottom Riding Club, circa 1948. Amid the dusty expanse of Muroc, it represented a place where people could eat, drink, dance, and otherwise enjoy an evening out. (Air Force photo)

A: Yes. Anything that was a good reason to have a party. (laughter)

Q: Do you recall any specific parties?

A: Not really. There were a number of them, it's safe to say. I did remember a convention coming there. It was the Aviation Writers Association. They were there on a Saturday as I recall. They flew up and saw the base then came over to Pancho's in the afternoon. This was the time I saw a DC-3 land on Pancho's airstrip. Our own peons were out with them so we had joined them. It was quite a party. She had brought some additional girls up from Hollywood. Again, as far as I am concerned, there was no hustling going on here. They were there and they were company. As far as any sex, I can't comment one way or the other. I do know one thing, they were all in bikinis of the times. Pretty soon some of them started taking their bras off. They were sitting on the fence and sitting by the pool modeling and being photographed. Finally, some of them took their bottoms off. They were photographed and so forth. I'll never forget this one guy, he was a Texan, I used to know his name. He had on a blue gaberdine suit, coat and tie and everything. One of the girls was sitting across the pool. He walked down the steps, into the pool and walked over to her, fully dressed. His clothes came out soaked. There was quite a bit of drinking that day. Beyond that, if there was, I don't know.

Q: It's well known that Pancho had hostesses there, especially, to attract the single people. I've heard that some of them were really lovely.

A: One of them, in particular, was. You see here again, these girls also served as waitresses in the dining room. Pancho used to say, "I don't know what they do after 2:00 a.m. I didn't hire them for that. I hired them to be waitresses and hostesses. Anything beyond that, they are on their own after 2:00 a.m." That was her position on that.

Q: Going back to the party with the Aviation Writers' Association, I'm trying to recall that there was one group that wanted to go to Pancho's. Do you know if this was group? I think it really irked General [J. Stanley] Holtoner, who was the Center Commander at the time. He couldn't believe that a group would actually want to go to Pancho's.

A: I don't know if Holtoner was General then or if Boyd was still there. I don't remember.

Q: You were saying that Pancho got along real well with General Boyd. From what I understand, it was a very different relationship with General Holtoner.

A: Very cold, or hot, whichever way you want to describe it. He started off as I said before, she went over to call on him as she did on every new commander. She walked into his office and she says, "General Holtoner, you know who I am." He said, "Yes, you're the lady who picks up the garbage." You know that didn't go over very well with Pancho. He was the only one she had a problem with. She and Gilkey were at sort of an arm's length but no real battle. She and General Boyd were very good friends. Boyd came out to give her away at her wedding.

Q: Were you there at the wedding?

A: No. I don't remember being there, but my wife says we were there. I just can't remember.

Q: You were saying that people would go to Pancho's for parties and things. I also heard that people would just stop by there to have dinner.

A: Yes, we did that more than once and it was very good. Her steak dinners were excellent. They were very good. It was a good restaurant.

Q: I've heard that you could order anything from a full coarse meal to just hamburgers.

A: That's right. It was ala carte.

Q: Going back to General Holtoner. One of the assignments that he was tasked with was to expand the base and modernize it.

A: He was following Colonel Gilkey's Master Plan, as a matter of fact.

Q: As a result of that, a lot of land surrounding the base was bought up.

A: The idea was to have a throughway from the [Rogers] Lake to Rosamond Lake. There was nothing in between.

Q: Pancho's property was smack in the middle of all of that.

A: That's right.

Q: Pancho felt that the government wasn't offering her a fair price for her property. She went to court over that. She also sued General Holtoner.

A: That was a different case. There were two different cases.

Q: I'd heard that Pancho requested that you testify at one of those cases.

A: It was the latter one. It's quite a story. Cliff Morris was involved. It started with a young lieutenant writing to the General and saying, "This Pancho's place was terrible. It was immoral and leading young lieutenant's astray, etcetera, etcetera, and it should be closed." He said that he had been virtually attacked by women over there and insisted he go with them, go to bed and so forth. He felt that this was just terrible for young lieutenants and it should be closed. Incidentally, I don't think this young lieutenant was a pilot. (laughter) So, there was publicity on this. He [General Holtoner] threatened to make the place off limits.

Pancho then sued him for defamation of character, that he was saying things about her that she was running a house of prostitution and so forth. She wasn't and so on and so on. She sued Holtoner for $1,000,000 for defamation of character. She couldn't get him to court. She just couldn't serve papers on him. She had Cliff Morris who worked for me and worked for her at night. He worked in my instrument shop. She knew Holtoner's movements. He was always leaving by air. She knew that he was going to leave this particular morning. Cliff was down there and served papers on him. I got an immediate call from the Judge Advocate. "One of your employees has done a horrible thing!" I said, "What has he done? I'll have to look into it." I stalled him as much as I could. When I looked into it, I found that he [Cliff Morris] was on annual leave and had served the papers. Meanwhile, they took his badge away. He had to sign in and out everyday. They also told me that they wanted me to fire him. That's when I started the routine of, "Send me something in writing."

Q: General Holtoner was so upset because he had been served a summons that he wanted Cliff terminated.

A: That's right. Once he had delivered the papers, there was a court trial set up. We were trying to do this in an orderly fashion but there was so damn much going on. Cliff told me that she wanted me to come to court and testify about what had happened to him. I said, "For god sakes, talk her out of it." We'd had so much going on. This was the year that we built the new [NACA] building. It's the central building out there at Dryden. We were dedicating the building in June [1954]. They had a very auspicious group of people coming out to witness the dedication. People like the Chief of the Air Force, Chief of the Navy Bureau of Aeronautics, Mr. Glenn R. Martin, Grover Loening, who had been an early pioneer of airplanes, Lester Gardner, who had founded the Institute of Aeronautical Sciences, people of this order. What we had done, we had quite a ceremony and then we had a buffet luncheon and a dance party like a ball that night in the hangar with an orchestra and floor show. The way we financed that was the every employee contributed to it over a year or a year and a half period. I forget the exact amount of money, but they all contributed to having this. It worked out very well. I remember when I told John Pickery who was the executive secretary of NACA what we were doing he said, "Fine. You arrange the party and I'll get the guests." This is how he got these people there. Of course, they had the three center directors of the other three NACA centers. It was quite an affair.

Pancho, meanwhile, was going to haul me into court and I could see it was coming right in the middle of all of the ceremonies and getting ready for it and recovering from it. I said, "Tell her to knock it off." He said, "No, I can't." He came back and told me, "She is determined." This was about a week before the celebration. My wife and I had gone down to get ice cream and bring it back for the kids. When we got back, the kids said, "There were some people here looking for you." From the description, I knew it was Pancho and Mac [Eugene S. McKendry, Panchos' husband]. I said, "Let's go to bed." (laughter) Which we did. At about 1:30 in the morning there is a knock on the door. "Walt Williams, I know you're in there. You might as well just answer the door. I'm going to keep knocking." It was Pancho. I got to the door and she said, "You remember me?" I said, "Yes, Pancho, I know who you are." She says, "Just what did happen with Cliff Morris?" I described it. She says, "Would you like to repeat that in court?" I said, "No." With that, Mac gave me the summons. I said, "Now look, you're getting me into a helluva bind here because we've got this big party coming up and as soon as it's over with, I'm taking off. I haven't had a vacation in 3 or 4 years. As soon as this is over with, we're going off for 3 weeks." She says, "What days are you available? I'll work you in." Which she did. We got down there to the court. In fact, I took my wife with me because she wanted to do some shopping to get ready for the trip. In those days, if you did any real shopping, you did it in Los Angeles. There was nothing available in Lancaster. Of course, all my Air Force friends were there, including Colonel [Howard C.] Knapp who was a medic [hospital commander] and others. Pancho saw me sitting with them. She said, "I want you over here." Just as I had gotten on and started testifying, the judge's wife stuck her head in the door and gave him the "high sign" and he said, "Why don't we recess for lunch? We'll be back at 2:00." I told my wife that I would meet her in the downtown Bullocks, as a matter of fact, for lunch. Pancho said, "I want you to come to lunch with us." I said, "Why?" She said, "I don't want you going with the Air Force. They will want you to change your story." I said, "No, Pancho, I'm not going with the Air Force. I'm going to go with my wife." "Are you sure?" I said, "Yes, she is waiting for me right now." "Well, if you are doing that, then it's all right." We went through the whole routine with the judge. "Who shot John?" That type of thing. I was finished then. I don't know what she got. I'm not sure she got more than a dollar out of the suit. Mac could tell you better. I know she didn't get a $1,000,000. She did get an adjusted bid on the property. I don't remember the exact numbers, but I know she got more than they originally offered her.

Q: What do you recall about her property? What all she had there. You mentioned the swimming pool and the airport.

A: She had this motel which, I'm guessing, had [20] units. It wasn't real big. She had the swimming pool and then a building with the restaurant and bar in it. She had an airstrip with a small hangar. She had some stock. I know she had pigs because that is why she was getting the garbage [to feed the pigs]. She raised alfalfa which was a big crop in this valley. I don't know the exact acreage. It was not small.

Q: When you went to Pancho's, you were saying that she had good meals and things like that. I've heard that she had what she called the "Happy Bottom Riding Club". If you got membership in that, then things were supposed to be cheaper. Was that the case?

A: I don't know. There was a gag for a lot of our Eastern visitors to have them become members of the "Happy Bottom Riding Club". I don't know.

Q: She had horses out there, too.

A: She had horses, yes. These were riding horses.

Q: One thing I've heard, too, I think it was on Wednesday nights, that used to be a big night for dancing and stuff like that. Do you recall any of that?

A: That's all kind of vague to me. I'm going to say, "From time to time, she tried different kinds of promotions to get people in to spend money."

Q: One of those promotions was the rodeo. I think she had an annual rodeo.

A: I think she did. I never went to it.

Q: Pancho was pretty generous with people she liked.

A: Oh yes, she was.

Q: Do you recall any specific instances of her generosity?

A: I know that she helped Cliff Morris buy his house. Whether she loaned him the down payment or made the down payment, I don't know. I know she helped him.

Q: It seems that Pancho's friends were very loyal to her, too.

A: Yes, they were. She was irascible. People would get upset with her from time to time.

Q: I think she was somewhat of an actress. She would put on this rugged image but if you got to know her, she would calm down.

A: I think that is right, yes.

Q: There were a lot of people who used to hang out at Pancho's because Pancho knew a lot of people from pilots to movies stars. Did you ever notice or run into any people like that when you were there?

A: I probably did, but I just don't remember any of them at this point in time.

Q: Pancho just loved pilots, whether they were military or civilian. How did she relate to other people, like flight engineers?

A: It depended on the individual. Either she liked you or she didn't. It depended on the personality of the guy.

Q: One thing I would like to get into a little bit. You mentioned that General Holtoner wanted you to fire Cliff Morris. I think you told him, "Well, write me a letter about it." Did he ever do that?

A: No, as a matter of fact, he didn't. Every time I would see him for any reason or other, he'd ask me if I still had that man on the payroll. Finally one day, this is the climax, he asked me if I had ever fired that man. I said, "No, I can't" He said, " What do you mean, you can't?" I said, "He works for you." He [Cliff] was working in the Air Force instrumentation shop. He [Holtoner] went critical. He called Paul Bikle in, who was the technical director of the Base at that time, and said, "Bikle, you have a 'commie' working in your shop." (laughter)

Q: So, when he found out that Cliff was actually working for the Air Force, he called him a "commie"?

A: Yes. He said, "In fact, that whole shop is full of 'commies'."

Q: I also understand that General Holtoner, allegedly tried to keep processors off the base.

A: That was true. That goes back to when I talked about he and the Judge Advocate coming to see me at the end of the day to tell me that he had given Cliff his badge back and didn't want to take any further actions right now, but later, they would want me to fire him. Again, I said, "Let me know." The reason he had done that was, they had been down in court that day. The judge just chewed them up and down and told him, "A military man cannot hide behind the reservation to avoid civil process. That's what you had been doing and that's illegal."

Q: I was a bit curious, did they try to make things tough for any other NACA people or was it only toward Cliff?

A: It was only Cliff. There were problems here and there. There always would be. Half of them were the NACA people's problems, too. They would get arrogant, too, but nothing serious.

Q: We have covered a lot of ground. Is there anything, before we conclude, that you would like to mention about Pancho or those early days that you were here with NACA?

A: It was a great adventure, I'll say that....A lot of things happened. I've only had that feeling several times in my life. That was one of them. Another one was when I was driving between Orlando and the Cape and knowing that before I left the Cape, we will have launched John Glenn. It was that same feeling.

SUBCOMMITTEE MEETS AT HSFS

The periodic meeting of the NACA Subcommittee on High-Speed Aerodynamics began Monday morning, October 1, with an inspection of HSFS facilities and aircraft and a demonstration, conducted by Wendell H. Stillwell (Research Engineering), of the jet control simulator.

Papers of interest to the Subcommittee, of which Station Chief Walter C. Williams is a member, were presented by HSFS Research Engineering personnel Hubert M. Drake, Richard D. Banner, Gareth H. Jordan, and Edwin J. Saltzman.

Concluding session of the three-day meeting, which was attended by over 20 committee members and delegates, was held on Wednesday.

HSFS RECEIVES BIRTHDAY CONGRATULATIONS

The following telegram was received this week by Chief of the Station Walter C. Williams: "Congratulations on the 10th birthday of the High-Speed Flight Station. May the next 10 years be as successful as the first."

Sending the message were J. W. Crowley, and I. H. Abbott of NACA Headquarters, and Dr. H. J. E. Reid, F. L. Thompson, and H. A. Soule' of Langley Laboratory.

The High-Speed Flight Station came into being in September 1946, with the official appointment of Mr. Williams as Station Chief in August 1947.

From the pages of the X-Press.

Clyde Bailey

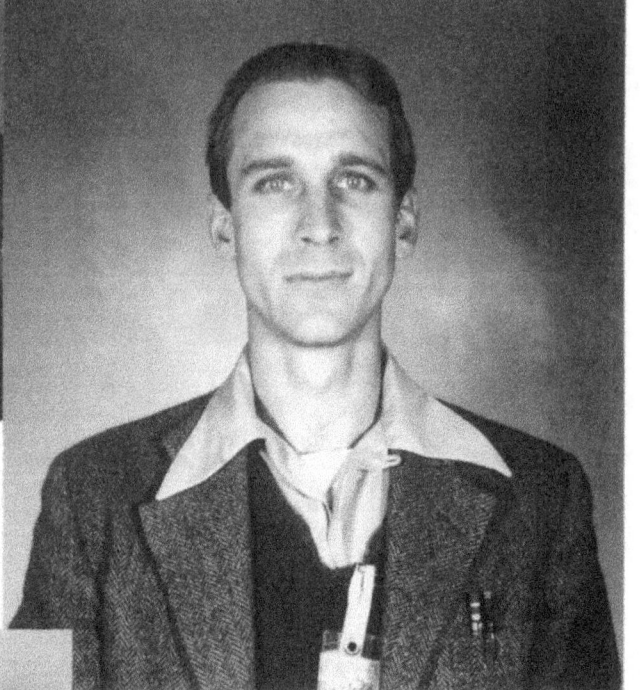

Don Borchers

Richard Cox

Ralph Sparks

CLYDE BAILEY, RICHARD COX, DON BORCHERS, and RALPH SPARKS

Interview by Michael Gorn, March 30, 1999

Although Walt Williams played a critical role as the center director, the men and women who worked for him actually made it a reality. They each followed different paths to Muroc - some had worked for the NACA at Langley Field, some heard about a job at Muroc, and some learned of opportunities through the military and the aviation industry. Tales of the early days at Muroc often stress the hardships, such as poor housing, unsanitary conditions, and the heat and dust. In contrast, this interview presents the other side of the story — the reasons why these men stayed while others left. They had been given a hard task, demanding long hours with minimal resources in spartan, isolated conditions. These shared hardships created a special bond that outsiders could not share. But the conditions would not remain indefinitely. The task ultimately required better facilities and more resources if they were to be accomplished successfully.

GORN: All right. I think what we'll do first is just go around to the four of the gentlemen assembled.

BAILEY: All right, Clyde Bailey. I'd like to make a comparison with working conditions at Langley Field and Muroc Army Air Base. At Langley Field, we had 95-degree days with 90-percent humidity. The humidity was so strong you thought it would rain. We came out here, and we had many hundred-degree-plus days, but the humidity was in the neighborhood of three to ten percent, which made it very pleasant. During the month of September, we could expect hurricane-force winds at Langley Field, which Don Borchers remembers correctly. Richard was also out there at Langley. It seemed that every September, we would have to fly whatever airplanes were flyable that we had out on the base somewhere else where they wouldn't be affected by the winds. Everything that was in the hangar, we had to jack up, take it and put overhead in the mezzanine floor that we had and jack up all the airplanes as high as you could get them off of the floor. Because there are high-water marks in the hangars at Langley Field that are as high as two feet.

So, at one time, all of Langley Field was covered with water. It must have [taken] them months to get the dead fish off of the Field. This was prior to when I went out there, but it was still something that we talked about. So conditions back there were not Shangri-La by any means. At Langley, we prepared for a hurricane each September. And, like I said, we had to move all of the equipment and the aircraft, and so forth. So we lost an awful lot of man hours back there. We never had to jockey the aircraft on the field at Muroc, and I don't recall ever having to fly those off because of high winds, do you?

BORCHERS: No.

BAILEY: Or have to jack them up or do anything else with them. As far as working conditions in the buildings were concerned, [in] the hangars at Langley, we had no heat in the wintertime. We had no air conditioning at all. Our hangars faced east and west at Langley Field so that we had full benefit of the wind going through there. We came out to Muroc, and we had heat in the offices adjoining the hangars, so you could go in there and get warm. In the summertime, if you got out of the sun, it wasn't too bad. But our living conditions were such that we had heat in the wintertime, all that we needed, and we had a evaporative coolers. We had none of that back East. It was just as hot in the house in the summertime as it was outside. The only thing you could do was open up the doors and have a lot of stationary fans around to blow through there. But it was a lot more comfortable here in the houses than it was back there. My home was four-and-a-half-years old when I came out here. The living conditions were probably, in some respects, better out here as far as climate control was concerned.

BORCHERS: Don Borchers. Do you want me to give you a brief summary of before I came out here?

GORN: Just a little bit, if you could.

BORCHERS: In March of 1941, I was working for the Glen L. Martin Company. I was a service rep on the Martin B-26. I first came across Langley when I went down there with the 22nd Bomb Group. And, incidentally, it was my first airplane ride. I was a new member, and I rode a flight in a B-26. It was a great experience. I didn't ever think that I would come back to Langley. But after I got out of Service, I had two jobs. I could go back to Martin on the flight line for $1.28 an hour, or I could come to Langley for $2,600 a year at NACA. I chose to come back to Langley. I really enjoyed my time at Langley because we could go down to the water and see all the aircraft carriers and catch a lot of fish and crabs and stuff like that. But to get back to here, Clyde had a New Year's Eve party, December of '47. And he asked me whether I'd want to come out to Muroc. I thought about it, and I came out here. And to get back to his things about the living conditions— He was perturbed about roaches? Well, when I came out to Mojave, we did have roaches. But I bought some spray and some roach powder. And in three days, our roaches were gone. Much different than we ever had back in Langley.

BAILEY: That's right.

BORCHERS: I lived in an apartment in Langley, and we never did get rid of those roaches.

BAILEY: That's right. No, in Virginia, you don't get rid of them.

BORCHERS: And those kind of things never bothered me a bit. Because I had just come back from the South Pacific where the roaches were about four inches long. The first days out here in Mojave, I really enjoyed. I went hunting for coyotes; you could see beautiful flowers; I saw flocks of quail. And I'd never seen these things before. It was just wonderful. We used to go up to Oak Creek, and they had wild horses running around. For a city kid, I really enjoyed it out here.

GORN: That was right from the beginning?

BORCHERS: That was right from the beginning.

GORN: Okay.

BORCHERS: I'll tell you one story. I was the first guy in Mojave to put a lawn in the front yard.

GORN: [Laughter]

BORCHERS: Yeah. Sure. Anyhow, getting back to this story. I'd come out from working [and] I would go out dig in the hard ground and do just a little bit. Well, one day, it had gotten dusk, and I was still working. I felt something up my leg, and I just swatted it; I didn't think [and] kept on working. When I went in to take a shower and put my pants down, the whole leg was red, violent red. So I said, "My God, what the hell is happening to me?" So I got a flashlight and went outside and looked around, and I found this great big, hairy spider. I didn't know what it was, so I put it in a can. Because over at the base, they had a corpsman. I took it down to his place, and I showed it to him. He told me it was a tarantula. Anyhow, he said, "I'll tell you what you do. You go back home. If you get sick during the night," he said, "I'll take you up to Tehachapi where they have a hospital."

GORN: Well, good. That's a good start. And thank you. Rich Cox?

COX: I was a local guy. I'm originally from Santa Monica. And after I got out of the Air Force, I went back to school. When I got through with school, somebody told the class that these people at Muroc had two openings [and] were looking for people in aviation. And I thought, "Gee, Muroc." And I can remember, the local, southern California guys used to run roadsters at Muroc on the dry lakes, back when I first became aware of automobiles. They would go run in there. One of the big things was when they hit a hundred miles an hour out there. So I said, "Well, I'll go up and give this a shot." I went up and interviewed with Clyde and some of the other people and, fortunately, I was hired. We were talking about salaries. I think Don said $2,600. I think I hired on at $2,400, something like that. But, gee, that was like all the money in the world, when I was a single guy, especially. But, to get back to the point, I came from Santa Monica, and it was very well developed. Now, at the time I came to work out at Muroc, there were probably—what?-3,500 people in Lancaster, something like that.

BAILEY: About that.

COX: About that. And I have no idea how many were in Palmdale. But everybody was aware—locals, southern California people, knew where Lancaster was and knew where Mojave was and knew where Palmdale was. But it was out in the desert, and you recognized that. However, at no time when I first went to work here did I have any feelings of being isolated. And, again, as Clyde pointed out, I found lodgings in Kerosene Flats. It was great for a single guy. I mean, everything you wanted was there, so there was really no problem. And then, of course, things improved. One of the things was I got married, and we moved into Lancaster, and so on. On a personal basis, that was all good, as far as I can see. And just as a point of information, for whatever it's worth—and I don't care how you use this—but I can honestly say that in the 28 years or whatever it was that I worked for NASA and NACA there may have been 50 times that I didn't feel like I wanted to go to work in the morning. I don't know how many people would say that about a job that lasted as many years as it did for me. So it was just a great situation as far as I'm concerned.

GORN: Was that part of the attraction—was the love of the work and a sense of the importance of the work?

COX: The camaraderie and working with the—I think, when I hired on with Clyde, I was number 26.

BAILEY: In the whole group.

COX: So, you know, we were like that size, 25, 26 people. That included everybody from Walt Williams on down. So it was a tight team, and it was a good team. It was great. I talk, now, to young aeronautical engineers, and I think, "These guys are all going through the same experience." And they can't believe the things we did. Not because of the magnitude of the things we did but the way we were able to do it without reams of paperwork and all kinds of reviews and those kinds of things. If it had to be done, we got it done, because it had never been done before. And that was part of the attraction, I think. You felt like you were helping to plow some new ground.

BORCHERS: I want to emphasize that. We had no safety rules, none at all. I can't hear high-pitch sounds now, because going up there and listening and looking around at a rocket engine, a jet engine and it's all gone. When the rocket was running, I'd get up on the tail, look in there, the damn fillings in my teeth were shaking. And we had absolutely nothing, no earmuffs.

BAILEY: Don [Borchers] was our first safety officer out at Muroc. And when Don left after many years, Richard [Cox] became in charge of all safety.

BORCHERS: Mmmm hmmm.

BAILEY: With about five or six individuals working under you.

BORCHERS: Yeah.

GORN: Ralph? Sir?

SPARKS: Ralph Sparks. I didn't go to work for NACA until 1950, but I'd worked for Northrop. But, prior to going to work for Northrop, I was with Douglas. And they occasionally used Muroc for flight testing. They were running the A-20 and a later model. But the main thing was that after war was declared, the cadets were flying P-38s out there. And after I went to work with Northrop, they always had some project going. So if an airplane was available, two or three of us would jump in and come up here in the morning to eat breakfast with the cadets. Because they got ham and eggs, and we couldn't buy that anyplace. But in 1950, I left Northrop and went to work with NACA. We lived in the old BOQ out there on North Base. Dick and I sometimes would take off and go someplace else to eat, but we had our own cook there—most of the time. The food on the base there wasn't bad. And the environment and the work—you worked as a group. The group was fairly well established. And you felt at home

From the pages of the X-Press.

EMPLOYEES INJURED SLIGHTLY IN EARLY MORNING ACCIDENT

Early Thursday morning two HSFS employees, Homer Hall and Roger Barnicki, experienced a freak accident while traveling from the NACA hangar to the unconventional fuels area to pick up peroxide for an early take-off of the X-1B airplane.

Leaving the hangar at 5 a.m., they proceeded along the usual route and found a barricade had been placed across the access road normally used to gain admittance to the fuels area. This made it necessary to retrace their route to get to the area from a different access road.

On the return trip a telephone trunk line suddenly loomed up in the headlights of the Weapons Carrier, completely blocking the road at about radiator height. Because of the short distance and the heavy combined weight of the Weapons Carrier and Peroxide Trailer, it was impossible to stop in time. The cable was picked up under the left front fender of the vehicle, which rode the cable pulling over three more telephone poles until it finally jackknifed into the ditch. Both Hall and Barnicki were thrown out of the driver's side of the vehicle and landed against the ditch bank.

Examination at the Base Hospital disclosed Hall and Barnicki sustained painful bruises.

Clyde Bailey headed an accident investigation committee, appointed by Joe Vensel, with Russell Mills and Harold Richards acting as investigators. Preliminary investigation with the NACA and Air Force determined that a class 7 pole failed between the time the vehicle first passed under the cable and the 15 minutes it took to return. Failure of the other poles resulted from the vehicle riding the cable.

right away, with Dick and Don and all. Why, you were one of the crew. We all worked together. If somebody had a project going and needed some extra help, you went over and helped them. It didn't make any difference what your classification was; if they wanted wires pulled in an airplane, you pulled wires in the airplane. It was a fun place to work, and I really enjoyed it.

BORCHERS: Well, let me emphasize something on the early days. I made it out to Muroc, December the 11th, 1941, in a DC-2. I got out of that thing, and I just had a Homburg hat and a camel-hair coat on. The wind hit my Homburg and it flew. I chased that hat for around two miles until I finally got it. But, anyhow, to get back, I was traveling with the 22nd Bomb Group. They were flying anti-submarine missions off the coast. And talk about conditions then: we ate off of just boards and, mostly, you just had hot dogs and cheese for about five days. They hadn't set up the tents, so they put me in a barracks, or bachelor offices quarters, the only building on the base then. They gave us sleeping bags.

We could hear the little flying wings, but I never could see it. It never came above the mountaintop all the time we were there. That was a little rougher. Some first lieutenant—his wife had driven him out at Christmas time, he'd take me to Hollywood. And the week before Christmas, he took off with three 500-pound bombs and went in. We picked up five—seven guys and put them in bushel baskets. Rough, rough, rough, rough.

GORN: When was that?

BORCHERS: That was December the 18th, 1941.

GORN: You say, 1941, it was a little rough. When does it start to really become where that's no longer [true]? You've got camaraderie with the group. Is it as the NACA team comes out?

BAILEY: Well, Northrop was established out here before we got out here. So I would say, starting in probably 1942. So Muroc started to become more habitable. I think Muroc was under March Field, right? Originally?

SPARKS: Yeah. Things started building pretty fast there after we got to the into the war. They started building barracks there, prefabs, and, of course, they built the O Club [Officer's Club] in '42. I don't know, it wasn't that bad. I wouldn't want to do it now. There was certainly no air conditioning. Whenever I was staying on the base, I always wanted to work out in the gym. They did set up a nice gym there for us. There was no air conditioning, and you'd go over there in the afternoon—it had been locked up all day—and open that up; you had to take the windows out. They didn't open, so we'd take them out. It was two stories and the wind blew through there.

BAILEY: Speaking of air conditioning, we didn't have them in the automobiles, either.

SPARKS: No.

BAILEY: And that Oldsmobile I had didn't have a heater in it, either, did it?

COX: No.

BORCHERS: The cars had those old things we'd put on the side of the window. Plus we always had a canvas bag on the front.

Two views of the NACA Men's Dorm at North Base. Because of the long travel distances and limited housing in Lancaster and Palmdale, single NACA personnel usually lived on base. During 1953 and 1954, a double room in the Men's Dorm cost $3.69 every two weeks, while a single room went for $6.00. In contrast, renters paid $75 to $100 per month for a single bedroom apartment in Lancaster. Since the starting salary for an engineer at this time was only $3,410 per year, the dorm had its attractions. (E-431 and E-432)

COX: Something else, too, I was a flight engineer in the military on B-24s. And a flight came up, and somebody said, "Well, you're a southern California guy, would you like to go with this B-24 out to Muroc?" And this was the beginning of the war. I said, "Oh, sure." So, we labored through the skies and finally got to Muroc. The plane went over the south lakebed, and I looked down, and there were about four buildings on the south lakebed.

The guy said, "I think that's where we're going." I looked down; and the thought that entered my mind was, "How in the world can anybody live out here? I just can't believe they do that here." So we landed, and we were taxiing down and, pretty soon, here comes a jeep. The guy says, "You can't come down here, and he moved us. Here we were sitting in the middle of a great, big lake bed. He moved us out of that road, over here, so we could park and shut down the engines and stuff. But, at the time, I thought to myself, "Man, I just can't believe that anybody would live out here." And, so—what?—six years later, seven years later, there I was. It was a good experience.

GORN: Because we talked about camaraderie – how important it was – could anyone talk a little about Walt Williams and what his role was in bringing people together, the kind of a leader he was?

BAILEY: It seemed like every project I got on, Walt was the project manager. I was on two or three projects with him back at Langley Field. Then, when the XS-1 program came along, Walt was involved in that. Before NACA accepted the airplane, he would fly back and forth to Niagara Falls to the Bell Corporation. Then, when the airplane became flyable, Walt and four other people went down to Orlando and did a few drops down there which were not too successful. He wipes a boundary marker and some other things because the visibility of the field was not very good from the air. So, that's when they decided that they would bring the vehicle out here. I came out in the first of November—Mel Gough and Buckley and myself. We flew a C-45 out here. Walt left at the same time in a Chevrolet automobile, and he brought [LeRoy] Proctor with him. He was an instrumentation man.

So I worked with Walt when he was actually just a young guy practically out of college. So I've known Walt for a long, long time. But he got housing out here. And when we came out here as families, we got the Marine base housing. It wasn't long after that that Walt moved into that. I think he was pretty much responsible for the Wherry housing out at the base, which was the first new housing built after the war. So Walt was pretty much responsible in that respect. He was a gung-ho individual. I don't think that he ever thought there was anything that he couldn't do. Nothing seemed to stop him. He was particularly concerned about safety. Whatever you were going to do, you had to show that it was safe for the other men. Don has been a friend of Walt and Helen for many years. If you, Don, if there is some input you would like to make.

BORCHERS: Don Borchers. I'll tell you about Walter. He was a real good friend of ours. And Clyde happened to mention about the O Club burning down? Well, Walt and Helen took Margaret and myself, and Harold Minichek and his wife; out to the O Club. Walt took his brand-new Ford. On the way out the float in the carburetor was acting up. Well, we got about to Ma Greene's place, and the damn thing quit on us. I got out there, and I hammered on the carburetor, and the float came up. And we were able to get into the base. So we went to the dance, had a great time, came out— Harold Minichek had had too much to drink— We couldn't get the damn car started. So I took the carburetor apart. I was handing the screws to Harold to hold, and, unbeknownst to me, he was throwing them over his shoulder. So when I tried to put it back, I couldn't. Well, here it was, two o'clock in the morning; the whole parking lot was empty. So Walt said, "What are we going to do?" I said, "Well, I think maybe I can coast over to NACA and steal the weapons carrier. I get over there, and the damn weapons carrier, from the ignition switch to the coil, had a great big, heavy, spiraled cable on the top of it. I was able to break it and get the two wires together. I had to be crunched under the dash holding the damn thing to the switch while Walt drove. I held that thing all the way to Mojave; the girls were freezing; Minichek is passed out. Well, early the next morning, we got the word that Walt had to go out to the base because his car was still out there, and they thought he had something to do with the fire. We had a lot of fun with him.

BAILEY: Clyde Bailey. Speaking of Walt's Ford and the problem that Don and Walt had with that stupid car. My uncle was a Ford dealer back in Hampton, Virginia, and Walt had bought a new car from him. I don't know if that was the one he brought out here or not. But, anyway, along the same lines, somebody put a radiator cap on Walt's gas tank. He lost the [gas] cap, and somebody put a radiator cap on. Well, he also tripped down the road. But what happened was, since the tank wouldn't vent-the vacuum, of course, was real strong—and it collapsed the whole tank. He wondered why for a while. He said his car was getting such poor mileage. He'd fill it up, but it only held about five gallons.

From the pages of the X-Press.

COX: Rich Cox. Now, my experience, not being one of the original group that came out here— Walt Williams was the boss, and I knew he was the boss. However, I have to say this, that because, I think, of the size of the group and, also, again—I keep coming back to this word—the camaraderie of the group, I never felt like I was a new employee. I never felt like I had to work my way up the system, and so on, and so forth. I was made to feel welcome. Walt was one of the people who was down on the hangar floor with you all the time. And if there was any problem, I would never hesitate. You could go to Clyde or go to Don or whoever, and hoped—and I knew it would get to Walter. He was a people person, Probably, I think, that's as good a description as I can think of. He was followed by other directors who had— Oh, I don't know, their skills maybe were different. But my feeling was [that] we were coming into a group that was already established. But as I look back now, I think that Walt was the right person in that job at that time.

BAILEY: Yeah, I'd like to amplify on that a little bit, too. My name is Clyde Bailey. What we didn't have out here was a caste system. Back at Langley Field, if you were down on the floor, and you went up and spoke to the pilots, they'd say you were brown-nosing. If you went to speak to Mel Gough [chief pilot and head of flight test at Langley] they said you were brown-nosing. These were friends of ours, you know? I was never exposed to anything like that before I worked for the government. That was something that I could never understand. I put six and a half years into that field. It was the same when I left, and I'm sure it's probably same today.

SPARKS: Worse.

BAILEY: Probably. But we came out here and, like Dick and Don and Ralph said, we all worked together. Hell, Joe Vensel

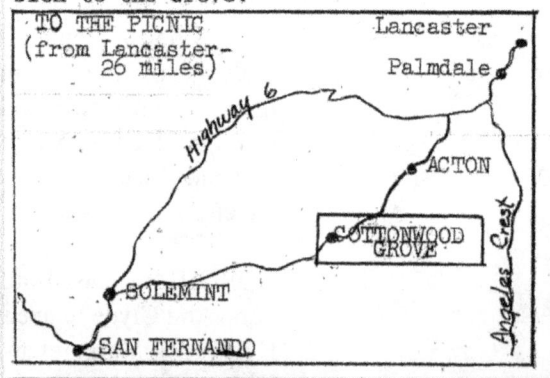

PICNIC DATE SET

Sunday, August 19, will be fun-day for HSFS'ers as the annual Station picnic gets in full-swing at Cottonwood Grove in Soledad Canyon (see map below).

The outing will be a "bring-your-own food" event, with beer, soft drinks, and cups furnished FREE. Cooking facilities (for roasting weiners, etc.) are available in the Grove.

Swimming, volleyball, organized softball, and horseshoe pitching will be featured activities for those who wish to participate.

During the picnic, the winner of the ice cream freezer, being raffled by the Activities Committee (see page 2) will be announced.

A small charge will be made for admission to the Grove.

Wanted: couple of old men to stand around 2nd and 3rd base on softball nights. Seriously, the enthusiasm is holding up well. Watch for the first league game date.

Anyone for tennis? Perhaps there are enough for an NACA tennis club.

The 1949 NACA annual picnic. Because of the isolated conditions and shared hardships at Muroc, the NACA personnel came to think of themselves as a family. This resulted in a number of group traditions, such as the yearly picnic, the softball, and the bowling teams. (E 236)

WANTED......SOFTBALL PLAYERS

Sign-ups are now being taken for a Station softball team to participate in the Lancaster League. All interested employees are urged to sign the sheets posted on the bulletin boards signifying position preferred, ie., outfielder, infielder (not 1st), first baseman.

For further information regarding the team, see Al Brown or Lloyd Walsh.

PICNIC ADMISSION PRICES REDUCED

By special arrangement with the management of Munz Lakes Resort, a reduction in the price of admission to the annual Station picnic on Sunday, September 18, has been effected. Upon presentation of a dinner ticket at the grounds entrance, adults will be admitted for 35 cents, children 25 cents. (Standard admission price is 45 cents for adults, 35 cents for children.) The admission charge covers use of the barbeque area, swimming pool, playground, and baseball diamond during picnic hours from noon to 8 p.m.

Boating, fishing, and horseback facilities will be offered at additional cost.

At 5 p.m. a barbecued chicken dinner will be served by Al Houser. Tickets for the dinner--$1.50 for adults, $.75 for children--should be obtained from Activities Committee members not later than Monday morning so an accurate count of persons planning to attend may be established.

Map directions and additional information on Munz Lakes Resort have been posted on Station bulletin boards.

TENPIN TALK

A four-game winning spree last night put Cotton Pickers into first place in the NACA Mixed League with 40 wins and 28 losses. Schizofrantics, former league leaders, dropped into second slot with 38 wins and 30 losses. Brown & Company took four forfeit games from Three Hits & A Mrs. to maintain third position.

STANDINGS

Team	W	L	Avg.
Schizofrantics	38	30	
Ernie Cadle			156
Harriet DeVries			130
Beverly Russell			115
Don Reisert			104
Brown & Co.	33 1/2	34 1/2	
Allen Brown			148
Terry Larson			151
Paula Truesdell			94
Dale Reed			121
Cotton Pickers	40	28	
Peg Sutphin			97
Don Hallberg			122
Dan Riegert			151
Joe Babine			128
Three Hits & A Mrs.	24 1/2	43 1/2	
Norman Musialowski			137
Pat Musialowski			102
Rex Cook			108
Harry Curley			135

From the pages of the X-Press.

would come down and help us change tires. And he was in charge of flight operations. Walt would do the same thing. There was never any distinction. Our grade against their grade. Right now, if you go to Washington, [and] some guy is a GS-15, you're supposed to take your hat off to them, you know? And we didn't have that.

BORCHERS: This is Borchers. And just to go back on that with Walt. We had a poker game every week with Walt. A few people would come out and play and Joe Vensel and myself. And we had a good time. But, one thing that threw me for a loop— Just a couple of years ago, Dick Payne, who used to be one of the crew chiefs on the X planes—we were just talking about playing poker, and he said, "Well, you were in a different class." And it never entered my mind that I was in a different class, that I was playing poker with the big guys.

COX: Rich Cox— As Clyde said, I was back at Langley with the B-47 with a couple of other people from out here and really ran into the caste system that Clyde described at Langley. This is not to put it down; it's just, that was the way the system worked back there. The three of us very, very obviously avoided getting in a buddy-buddy relationship with anybody because we never knew which way it was going to go. We got to know whose side these people were on, you know? This was really a tough go. It wasn't a comfortable feeling because we were used to something better. What I felt was better.

SPARKS: Getting back to Walt, I was working for Northrop, and we had the X-4 airplane up here and running tests on it. It was going to be turned over to the Air Force, and the Air Force was going to loan it to NACA. One day, I went out to the airplane, and here was a couple of guys climbing over it and looking at it. I asked them if I could help them. Walt introduced himself, and he was all questions. They spent the whole afternoon there just going over that airplane. I had one big complaint about the airplane from a safety standpoint, and I'd mentioned it to Walt. Never thought anything more about it. A short time later, the project ended, and the airplane was transferred to NACA, and I decided to transfer, too. Went down there, and, right off the bat, Walt strolled into Vensel's office, and he said, "Explain your worry about the airplane." I said, "Well, the problem is the speed flaps on it. The lefts and rights are operated from different hydraulic systems. If you lose one hydraulic system and you open that speed brake, you're going to tear the tail off. The chief structural engineers informed me of that, and I worry about it." He says, "All right, we're going to fix that." And, by golly, before NACA ever flew the airplane, they tore it apart and replumbed it.

BAILEY: Sparky would probably take issue with me. Clyde Bailey. Sparky brought an airplane over. And one of the engineers evidently preserved eggs. Because they had leaks in the fuel tank, so what they did was put water glass in the wings and sloshed it around. That worked fine for a while, but after a while, it kind of dried out and started peeling off. It filled up all of the filters and everything else. We never did cure those leaks.

SPARKS: Nope. And, today, that would have been a very simple repair. The way the fuel system was set up in that airplane, the whole wing was a fuel tank. And they had a number of different strobe pickups, almost what was the bottom of the airplane, just so the fuel could fall in there and be sucked out. Or you'd get most of it out. You'd go in and flood the wing with sealant would have plugged those up. But we never did anything but try to do it from outside, and it never was right, never worked.

BAILEY: Let's get away from overhauling the airplanes and get back to what you want to talk about. We had none of my group leave due to the living conditions. Some of the personnel in engineering did, and it was for different reasons. In our group, two of them went to new jobs. As far as being on the base, we had full access to the O Club and the NCO Club. I feel it was just a very pleasant association that we had. We had use of the base swimming pool. There were also pools at Willow Springs. You won't find this today, but fresh water came in on one end and went out on the other end, so it was always perfectly clean. We had picnic areas at Willow Springs, and we had barbecues at the Duntley Ranch for the NACA personnel, which were very pleasant and something to look forward to. There were many entertainment functions put on at both of the clubs. One of them was the Stag Night that we had until we had some nurses come out there and cut the whole thing off. Sunday dinners—we looked forward to going out to the O Club—by both the single people and the families that went out there. We never observed or heard anyone complain that the conditions in either kitchen were unclean. I never heard that. If it had been, I'm sure we wouldn't have gone out there. So, that was available to us.

We didn't have to go to Vegas. At that time, we had slot machines out there on the base, so if you wanted to strengthen up your right arm, you had plenty of opportunity. The housing rents were reasonable at the Marine base. I think the basic rate was $45.00, and then whatever functions, the base took care of; they added a certain amount. So it ran about $51.00 or $55.00 a month. What was peculiar was, if you used the wash house at the base—which were for all the washing machines—that was included in your rent. But if you brought your own washing machine in, they increased the rent. Well, we had ours flown in from Langley Field on the old C-47. Don got one of the deluxe apartments, because he had an electric refrigerator. Ours had an ice box. And if you think it's not a problem, we would buy the ice out at the base, put it in the car and run like hell 17 miles, and we would have maybe three-quarters of that thing left when we got there. That was something we weren't use to. Transportation was no problem. I think most of us had our own vehicles. And since we were out here on government orders—and if you're familiar with government orders—you got transferred for one year at the convenience of the government. Well, in our case, the government never thought it convenient to send us back, so we were out here. But we thought we were only going to be here a year. After De E. Beeler and I came out here, we went down to Tijuana; we went up north, we went all over the country.

And when I went back and brought my wife out— Like I said, my uncle was a Ford dealer, so I got the first, new 1947 Ford off the Campatella Ford Ranch in Virginia and drove it out. And it was quite a deal because no one had seen a new automobile in four years during the war. So it was like some guy flying a wing on me. He'd pull up alongside and look the car over and everything. Drove down to Los Angeles. Figueroa was the big automobile street at that time. And these guys would run out from the dealership: "Hey, would you like to be a rich pedestrian?" All that stuff. It was quite a deal. Like I say, we went down to Mexico. The base theater had pretty much up-to-the-minute movies. And, also, there was a movie house in Mojave.

GORN: Excuse me. About what year did the theater open?

BAILEY: It was there when we got there, November of '46.

COX: One of the first things the military put in was the theater.

SPARKS: I know it was there in '43. I don't know how long before that.

BAILEY: Well, in addition to eating out at the base, Mojave had good restaurants. We had French's and—

BORCHERS: White's [Motel].

BAILEY: Yeah. In fact, I stayed the first week in White's Motel when I brought my wife out. They were fixing up the housing over there at the Marine base. Got there on the seventh of April, 1947, at White's Motel. I went in and took a shower, and I wondered why I was bouncing back and forth; everything was unsteady. I came out and looked, and you know what? She said, "I was doing something on the bed," and she said, "I thought I pushed the whole thing up against the wall." She said, "And I opened the door, and people were hollering, 'earthquake!'" So, that was our indoctrination to it.

BORCHERS: Welcome to California.

BAILEY: We had night clubs and all that stuff. And right behind the Marine base, there we lived we had a rodeo every year.

BORCHERS: Oh, yeah.

BAILEY: Every year. People came from all over to do that. There was a lot more there than what we left behind us.

BORCHERS: We had a thing called "Gold Rush Days"; open gambling, prostitution [laughter]. Now, I just want you to know that everything wasn't peaches and cream. I remember that in 1948, Washington's Birthday, the wind blew so damn hard for three days you couldn't even get out of the buildings. When it finally let up, the Highway Patrol were leading people from Barstow all the way through. The people had to lean out of their cars because they couldn't see out of the windshields. [and] all the paint was off of some of the cars. But during that storm, I had a knock on the door. I went there, and here's a guy with a gas mask on; he's carrying a little burner. LeRoy Proctor came to my house carrying a small gasoline burner. Our units were all electrical, so we had no way of cooking. I was always grateful to Proctor for that. We could have something to eat. But we did have to brush out about three inches of dust.

BAILEY: Well, that particular storm, I remember. It blew out one of the windows in our bedroom. We didn't have any electric, and we were happy to have the kerosene space heater. What Millie did was take a bunch of coat hangers and put them on the handle of the pot and lowered it down into the space heater so we could cook with it all right. That was the same night Walt and Helen Williams were over at our house. When that wind went across there, it sucked all of the light things out of the dump.

BORCHERS: That was the day that I had to go back to Buffalo with the X-1 in June. That's when we had that big storm.

GORN: A question here to Mr. Bailey about Mel Gough, what he was like as a person?

BAILEY: When I went to work for NACA back in 1941, Mel was the head of Flight Test. He was our chief test pilot. Mel was probably one of the most careful pilots I know of and probably one of the most knowledgeable test pilots in the country. I remember, before the B-19 flew, they wouldn't let it fly at Douglas until Mel came out representing an insurance company. So he was very much thought of; he was known all over the world. He would go back and forth to Europe periodically. He was very easy to get along with but very meticulous about what he did and very careful about what he was told. For example, he'd get a new airplane, and if you happened to be the crew chief, before Mel would fly it, he might be sitting in the cockpit, and he'd question you about different operations in that particular airplane. He would ask you things that you knew that he knew, probably, so that he could weigh your knowledge about the things that he didn't know when he asked you a question about it. So, that way, he had a sense of security. And he flew a lot of first flights on a lot of airplanes all over the country. He was a good friend of ours; I spent time at his home after he came out here. I would give

Mel more responsibility for the improvements that the NACA group got out here through his intercession than anybody else that was involved. And he did this all through Langley Field and contacts through Headquarters, as well. Headquarters was the very peak of the whole organization. So, most anybody just didn't get up there and complain or get favors.

GORN: Because he had the profile.

BAILEY: He had the profile to do that. And no one really crossed Mel Gough. When Mel left NASA he'd been down at Kennedy. But his heart was not in shooting something up in the air and then waiting to see what happened. He was more of a[n] aviation, flight-type individual, right? He left that to go to work for CAA, the Civilian Aviation Authority. He came out here on an investigation, something that happened out here to one of the airplanes. So he called me up, and we went over to the Riverside Inn. I met him over there. He said that he had this particular position with CAA, and he wanted me to come back there with him, back to Washington, D.C. So I told him that I would. I put my house up for sale. They would have started me at GS-15 back in Washington, which was above what I had here. But they were very insistent that I get back there right away, and I just didn't want to leave Millie, and we had the kids in school, and so forth.

GORN: Yeah.

BAILEY: So the opportunity passed me, but that was the only time I ever thought seriously about leaving NASA. So after he retired, he moved down to Melbourne Beach, Florida. And every couple of years or so, when Millie and I would drive back there. We had relatives in South Carolina, North Carolina and all the way down through the South. We spent time with Mel and his wife back in Florida. Mel was a good friend of ours. Let me tell you something. Just before Mel died, we went down to Fort Lauderdale; he had friends in Lauderdale. And we stopped by to see Mel to spend some time with him. Millie said she'd never seen him so upset. In Florida, your driver's license is automatically renewed; you have to just sign the paperwork, and so forth. But Mel let his lapse, and as careful as he is, he went and took the examination and failed it.

GORN: Here's more to follow on Mel Gough. Mr. Bailey, do you have more to add on him?

BAILEY: No, I think I'll let Dick go ahead and give you some of his impressions of Mel. Then Ralph and Don can go.

COX: I had heard of Mel Gough and, obviously, it was all good words from everybody I talked with. I had the experience of going back to Langley with the B-47 project. I was only back there about, well, a short time, and I think it was about a year altogether but off and on. But, anyway, one time, I was down on the hangar floor with a B-47, and they were doing some instrumentation work. Mr. Gough came down, and it was the first time I'd ever really talked with him face to face. He introduced himself, and I introduced myself. He knew me because he knew I was coming out there with the program. But, basically, the key to his attitude toward things, as Clyde pointed out, was— He asked me a question that—a technical question that I really didn't have the answer to. And I said, "I don't know, but I will find out." He said, "That's all I wanted you to say." That's the way he operated. And I did find out. Boy, I spent about four hours that night finding out, but I did find out. That's the kind of person he was. He just wanted to know—as Clyde pointed out, he wanted to know were you qualified to do what you were doing and did you have the right attitude.

GORN: And maybe test you on it.

COX: Yeah. Right.

BORCHERS: I first met Mel when I got out of the Navy in 1946, and came back to Langley. He called me up in his office, and we started talking about airplanes. And we got along pretty famously because he was from Baltimore, Maryland, and so was I. But I want to tell you one incident. I didn't find a caste system like these other guys did, I have to tell you. So, this one particular time, it was John Stack and a couple of other bigwigs and Mel, flew up to Washington to the Headquarters. I flew along as crew chief on the airplane. We landed at Washington National; they got out. Mel handed me the keys; I locked the thing; and I said, "What time will you be back?" He said, "so and so." So I got in a taxi cab, and I went to meet a friend of mine. I came back, and I waited until they came in. We got home; it was past time, everybody has gone, and I didn't know how I was going to get home. John Stack, the chief engineer, took me home. See, so different people see different things. As far as a caste system. They couldn't have been any nicer to me.

GORN: I understand that in the very early days, Walt Williams worked for Mel Gough and then later for Hartley Soulé.

BORCHERS: Mmmm hmmm.

GORN: If you just choose a few words for Williams versus a few words for Gough. Let's say, some of the hot temper, some of the placid. You know, can you have some words for what they were like, how to characterize them just a little bit?

BORCHERS: My impression— I don't think they were that much different.

GORN: Okay.

BAILEY: I don't remember Williams ever flailing his hands around or raising hell or anything. And Mel was pretty even-tempered, as well. One thing, I was with NACA for about two years, and I went to work for $1,800 a year. I was the first person hired in Flight in seven years. And two of us went in— a fellow named Sullivan. We were hired to go to Lewis Laboratories, the engine facility. I had an internal combustion engineering background, and they wanted to send us up to Lewis. By the time it came to go there, Mel wouldn't release us. So I got a hold of Mel one day; I said, "Mel, how about a raise?" I said, "Geez, I've been here a year and a half and haven't gotten a raise." He put his hand on my shoulder, and he said, "Clyde, flying is fun."

COX: That sounds right.

BAILEY: Also, Mel's brother— I don't know if you've ever heard of him— Eddie Gough—

GORN: Yeah.

BAILEY: Eddie was the last one out of Corregidor to carry a load of nurses with him. He was a Navy pilot. After he got out of the service, he went to work up at Lewis Laboratory. He was on foot. So Mel said, "Can you get Eddie a car?" Well, my uncle was in the automobile business, so I went out and got a car for Eddie.

GORN: What was Hartley Soulé like?

BAILEY: Well, I can tell you what I thought of him, and I can tell you what Chuck Yeager thought of him. It wasn't too long ago when Chuck came to the O club at Edwards. And we got talking about the early flight tests. And he said, "That damned Soulé. Do you remember him?" I said yeah. He said, "He cost me a year's worth of flying." He said, "Geez, you couldn't do anything." And at the time—and you can check this with [De] Beeler—the increment increase in mach number was such that, if they had had their way, the flight increase would have been in the neighborhood of 18 miles per hour. Now, you know, they would have still been testing right now at that rate. But, anyway, Soulé was very capable; he didn't come from the flight end of the Langley Field facility; he was more a tunnel-type individual. Tunnels were the big things back at Langley, and it became that way at Ames Laboratory, also. But Hartley, as far as I was concerned, from what I knew of him, did a real good job out here. And like Don said, he was friendly. He was kind of the leveling force as far as flight test was concerned. It was going to be done incrementally and not just gung-ho and lose another airplane or something along those lines like we did over in Ames. So, that was my impression.

BORCHERS: Borchers. My impression. I knew he was a very, very serious poker player. But on the humanitarian side, I have to tell you this, though. I had to leave NACA when I had a nervous breakdown. And when I was having problems, he did come to me and talk to me. He really wanted for me to get back there.

SPARKS: Ralph Sparks. I really never knew Soulé. I had the misfortune of meeting him kind of the wrong way. He was flying into LAX one afternoon, and John Griffith came down and asked me if I would get a vehicle. You know, he said, "Come on, be my co-pilot, and we'll go down in the C-45 and pick up the Great White Father. I didn't know who in the hell he was talking about. So we went down to get him, and he came out and set his bag down. So I ran over and picked up his bag and was going to carry it to the airplane. And, boy, he grabbed that out of my hand, and he says, "I carry my own bags. They don't have to do it for me." So that was my introduction to the Great White Father.

BORCHERS: There was no brown-nosing involved.

GORN: It sounds like the support back at Langley was very good. The set up by these people, anyway. I think De Beeler was saying that, also. That he in particular said Mel Gough and John Stack supported the effort out here very well.

BORCHERS: Well, I would think they would have to. Because, after all, it was their project, their baby, so—

SPARKS: Well, they certainly made it grow. There was a lot of good men from back there that made it a success.

BAILEY: Well, the reason it went so well is, we were pretty much on our own. We didn't have to get some engineer back in Washington to determine whether or not this is the next step. And we didn't have all of those problems, so it worked real well. Walt had the initiative and the background and the ability to go ahead and make decisions that were right. So it was great working that way.

COX: Going back to that same point—and I think I mentioned this once before. Since I've retired, I've had occasion to talk to a number of young aeronautical engineers. And there was one in particular who was really interested in those days. So, naturally, I wound up telling him stories about things that we did in those days, and not with the idea of glamorizing, just telling him that this is the way we were doing it. And he just kept shaking his head. I finally said, "What's the problem?" He said, "Do you know," he said, "if we were trying to do this today, we would start with a proposal, and we would call in the weight and balance people; we would call in the stress people; we would call in the hydraulics people, and so on, and so forth; and we would wind up with a stack of documents this high. Then it would go through review. By the time we got all through, we would have forgotten what we started to do to begin with." And I think that was the difference there. In those days—and I hate to live in the past like this—but in those days, that's why it was so much fun, I think. Because good people were doing good jobs. I don't know whether this is a true statement or not, but I think Clyde or somebody told me that Neil Armstrong said one time that the people at Edwards, the people at Muroc, do what they do, the best of any one in the world. And I can't think of a nicer compliment than that. And I think it's true.

BAILEY: Bailey. Talking about drawings, and so forth, when we came out here, the NACA people didn't like the arrangements of the instruments in the X-1. So Don got the privilege of going ahead and changing all of the instrumentation. And the only thing that was given to him was just a drawing with a bunch of circles on it and the name of the instrument and where they wanted it located. I think that's all you had until the thing was completed.

GORN: Basically, you had great latitude.

BORCHERS: Yeah. They just hand you something, and you do it, that's all.

BAILEY: One of the funny ones we had. This was an engineer that came up from San Diego, a big, tall guy. He was assistant to Joe Vensel. He sent a drawing down, and on the bottom of it, it said, "Shape for beauty." Sparky was in charge of our machine shop then. Okay, we were talking about vehicles sometime ago. We had a Beech C-45 aircraft, and I don't know where we got the old Dodge car from, do you? The girls had that.

BORCHERS: Oh, the old grey ghost?

BAILEY: That was it, and then we had a Ford station wagon and a scooter, and that was it. At the beginning, when we first came out here, they left the C-45 with us. I guess Don was involved in this, too. We tried to fly it every morning to work as a commuting thing. By the time we got the thing cranked up and warmed up and ready to go, we could have been there in the automobile. We never got the gear up; we would be over at Muroc before we had time for it. So we tried it for a while, but it just didn't work out at all. But where we were housed with the X-1 originally was in what they call the big hangars. They moved over to what's now the main base. Our crib was right adjacent to Howard Hughes. Because he had the XF-11.

BORCHERS: Right. And the crib we took over from Bell.

BAILEY: Right. You know, it was a good association. Because, back in those days, nobody had ever had everything they needed. You would just continually borrow from

this guy and that guy, and somebody was borrowing from you and— Howard Hughes would came in. And, one time, he brought old [Congressman] — Oh, what the hell was— A real short guy. Anyway, we all shook hands with him, you know? That was before he was afraid of being contaminated there. Or else we contaminated him, so he was more careful afterwards. So, anyway, it was a good association, and it was not too bad working in there.

BORCHERS: Yeah, they used to come in the crib. I had a huge screwdriver about that long. And I come back and went in the toolbox, and the damn thing was bent. I made myself a sign— "Which son of a bitch broke my screwdriver?"—and put it up on the cage. Frank Danis, the rep from Reaction Motors, told me he was. And he never replaced the screwdriver.

COX: That XF-11 was a beautiful airplane. I remember the guys spent all their time just polishing that thing, just polishing that.

BAILEY: That [Congressman] was named Pella. Yeah. That's when Hughes was promoting the "Spruce Goose." Pella was out there. Also, that airplane that he had next to us was the one that he went into Bel Air, wasn't it, in the golf course.

COX: Yeah, he put it in there. Yeah. He put it in and took out a lot of golf-course real estate.

BORCHERS: When Clyde was talking about the big hangar— For a while, we had both these X-1s before the Air Force decided they'd take over.

BAILEY: Yeah, we proved both of them. Well, that would be— Then Jack Russell came in. He was working for Bell—

BORCHERS: Jack didn't come in until 1950, to us.

BAILEY: Not to us. But he went to work for the Air Force. Jack was here at the early part on the P-59, but we didn't know him then. Walt arranged for us to move from where we were at the airport, the big hangar, to the Butler hangar. And what one of these things says is that the personnel from Ames came down here, some of their people, to put up the lean-tos or whatever you want to call them—the offices and the shops, and so forth, on both ends of the hangar. That wasn't the way it worked. We had a contractor come out there, and he put up all this stuff. What was different about that, and I don't know if it was being done in the war or not, but instead of using gravel as an aggregate in these walls that they put up and the roof, and so forth, they used volcanic ash. They mixed that in, which made it very light. And if you look at them, these pieces that they put across there, solid pieces of concrete, they would put a box inside it, a cardboard box. So when you looked at this thing, actually, what you had then was an I-beam, because they filled the void. And this was concrete around here. So it looked like it was an I-beam. Worked real good. And the volcanic ash that they used as the aggregate was a real good insulator. It made it cool in the summertime, and it was easy to heat it in the wintertime. And in the summertime, of course, you had the evaporative coolers in there.

There was something else that we had, we never mentioned. The C-47 would come out here almost on schedule. And, generally, they would bring us out something. And what we usually wanted or asked for was, "Bring us down a barrel of oysters." So they would bring out a great, big barrel of oysters. And over next to where we were living, we would have these oyster roasts at night. See, we often thought that, somewhere down the line, when people excavate this, they're going to say, "Well, this was one great, big sea at one time. Look at all these oyster shells."

COX: Yeah. Yeah, I remember sitting in the C-47 one time. Geez, I don't know where we were, but Walt was on board, too. And somebody brought out these cartons of chilled seafood. Walt said to me, "Did you ever eat any oysters?" I said, "Gee—" And Clyde goes, "No, no, no, that's not the way." He says, "Here," and he pulled one of these big, drippy oysters— He says, "You do it like this." Down it went. Anyway, the middle of the night, eating oysters in a C-47.

BAILEY: Bailey. We had rattlesnakes out here just like they had back in Virginia. However, the ones in Virginia were Timber Rattlers. Don can tell you about a rattlesnake. He had one on the front porch.

BORCHERS: Yeah, I'd like to tell you about it. We were sitting there eating our supper. My son was three years old, and he didn't want any dessert. He said he'd go out and sit on the porch. So he opened up the screen door and closed that screen door, sat down, got up, opened up the screen door and says, "Daddy, there's a snake out there." And here was a little sidewinder, one button and a little rattle on it. I just smashed it, I'm sorry, Rich.

BAILEY: One thing out here. When people thought about going back—that had children,—they would go back to Virginia on a trip or something, and then they would come back here and be really happy to be back. For the simple reason that we didn't have these little throw-away diapers and stuff like you have now. These were regular diapers that you put out on the clothesline, and you had a whole string of them. They would hang them on one end of the clothesline here, go all the way down to the end, come back and pick them back off the clothesline because they're dry and clean. Go

> FLIGHT LINES
>
> After several hectic days of "digging out" (brightened considerably by bankers' hours), work at the HSFS ski lodge returned to normal this week - - the snow-ma'am on the front steps melted, the ice plant de-iced, and "snow on the desert" became just another remember-when story.
>
> * * * * *

From the pages of the X-Press.

A mid-1950s street scene in Lancaster. Even with the growth of both Edwards AFB and the High-Speed Flight Station during the 1950s, Lancaster still remained a small desert town. Despite this row of storefronts, the primary activity in the Antelope Valley continued to be farming. (E-1787).

back there, and you're hanging them over the shower curtain and all that kind of stuff, and they're dripping there for three or four days.

COX: That is a quality of life issue.

BORCHERS: But to get back to his story of how you liked it out here, I was finally able to buy a 1948 Dodge, and I took a trip back to Maryland. We got back there, and it felt as if the streets were closing in on me, after being in the wide open at Mojave. Here, my next neighbor was— Well, we had a pig farmer, he was about a mile and a half [away]. But the next place out was Boron.

GORN: You get used to it?

BAILEY: Yeah, I had something. I insulted my sister-in-law. She came out, and I went down the hall. I said, "Well, you can tell somebody is from back East is here. You can smell it." And, boy, she took off. The pillows were musty smelling, you know?— particularly the pillows, and the bed clothes and everything. Here, you don't sweat on them; you don't lay in, you know, perspiration, and so forth. So it's quite attractive, in that respect, isn't it? You know, as far as sports are concerned, I think we all liked to see the snow, but we liked to see it up there on top of the mountain. If we want to go up there and play in it, we can. The kids liked it; we would take them up there, and so forth; but you didn't have to live in it.

BORCHERS: What got me one time— It snowed here about six or eight inches, and it closed everything down!

BAILEY: Oh, yeah.

BORCHERS: I couldn't understand it. Because back in Baltimore, you went to work whether it was 10 or 12 inches of snow.

SPARKS: In fact, Joe Walker and I were going to work one morning, and it had been snowing all night. It was probably four or five inches. We were going up Sierra Highway. And right where the old radio station is there's a little hook in the Sierra Highway. A car coming towards us spun out, and I swung off and got out on the curb. And, of course, we get off the pavement. We went around it and came back onto the highway. The hind wheels went around, and, so, I'm pointing the wrong way, and I said, "Well, I'll go down here and turn around." He says, "No, you don't." He says, "We're going home." We didn't go to Muroc that day. We went over to my house, sat and drank coffee and played Rummy or something. I don't know.

BAILEY: Speaking of Mojave, I gave a speech at the Marriott Hotel over in Alexandria on Davis Highway. I needed some background information. I was giving a speech to a reunion of people from NACA, and they had about 400 people. What I wanted was some factual information. So I called the library to find out the population in Mojave, Lancaster and Palmdale back in 1946. The best they could come up with was [that there] less than a thousand people in Palmdale; there was about 1,800 or 1,900 people in Lancaster. And there was probably twice that many in Mojave. Mojave at that time was larger, and I would say, half of them probably belonged to the railroad. Because Mojave had the big roundhouse there and a lot of the trucking and industry, and so forth, that went through there. So we weren't dropped into the smallest part of the area out here. At that time, Mojave was a pretty good size. Then, of course, the roundhouse went to Barstow, so we lost that.

Everybody likes to know about Pancho's. We went there occasionally. You could get a good steak. A lot of people came out from Hollywood, the so-called Hollywood starlets. A lot of the Army Air Forces people came out here, as well. You could go to Pancho's and get a good steak dinner. It could be a whole plate for a dollar. At least, at that time. It's probably equal to five or ten dollars now. They had a swimming pool there. We would go over there between one and two in the afternoon; we could go swimming. There was plenty of activities. She had horses that you could rent. That was one of Chuck's problems. He rented that horse and went into that fence before he flew supersonically. They had a nice, little air strip. Beeler kept his airplane there. Dick flew in and out of there. So that area was available to us. So we weren't exactly stuck out in the middle of nowhere with not anything to do.

COX: Well, let me check on that a little bit, the air strip. I flew in, in his airplane, a lot. We flew together at the time. And one night, De and I— What was his other plane? A Taylorcraft? But, anyway, a light aircraft-two-place. So we were up hanging around at night. And her strip was a long, kind of a sloping strip. The night lights were these pots that the strips used to use—

SPARKS: Smoke pots.

COX: Yeah, smoke pots. And she had them lined up along this [runway]. So De says, "Why don't you go ahead and shoot a landing?" And I said, "Okay. Fine." It was getting dark, and he said, "It'll be a good experience— You shoot one, and I'll shoot one." So I come in, and managed to get it on the ground without hurting myself or anybody else. And, so, we roll on through. And it was dark down there. So he said, "Well, let's do it again. Go ahead." I turned around and started taxiing back. And as I taxied back, there were four cattle going across the runway. They were going home. It was time to go home.

GORN: What timing.

COX: Yeah. They were some of Pancho's animals, and they were crossing right in the middle of the runway. And I guess, five seconds earlier, and we'd have a problem running into them. I mean, it was an experience.

GORN: That would help to get a little visual picture of what the [housing] were like to live in.

COX: This is Rich Cox. What little I remember about that Wherry was that when I went to work, I was single. And that makes, obviously, a world of difference. So where I went, I think, was called base housing. It was out of plywood, and as I remember—I know for a fact that you roomed with somebody—another guy.

BAILEY: Wasn't De with you?

COX: De and I roomed together. But this was a part of the military thing at that time. And, the only reason I don't remember much about it was because I ate and slept there and went to work. On weekends, I went on down below. So I didn't spend a lot of time there. And that's another point, too, that you might make of my situation. I was single, and I was a local guy. So almost every weekend, I drove down below. I had reason for going down below. And in the course of doing that, there were people who said could I give them a ride to L.A., and then you'd go to L.A., and so forth. And, so, it wasn't as if we were completely isolated up here and we didn't have anything to do. They didn't have the Freeway, and Sierra Highway could be a bear sometimes.

But, nonetheless, Roxie [Roxanah Yancey] and a couple of the woman [computers] would want to go down shopping, do something down below, over the weekend. So I'd drive them down, then pick them up on Sunday night, and we'd come back. So like I say, we weren't completely isolated. I wasn't. I was a roamer before I got married. That was a couple of years after I went to work for NACA. So, that was the difference with me. But the accommodations I had was—I think they called it government housing. I don't really [know] the name.

The reason I know it wasn't very well built was because my roommate and I had an altercation one time, and we knocked down the plywood wall. The wall came down. I got a new roommate, and we went from there.

SPARKS: You didn't hurt him that bad.

COX: I know. It was just an accident. Sort of.

BAILEY: When I came out here, I lived in the BOQ [Bachelor Officers Quarters]. And that was just to the west of the big hangars. They were two stories buildings. And everybody that came on base, whether they were military or what have you— It was the only BOQ that they [stayed]. Adjacent to that was a BOQ where the girls lived. It was right next door. It was a long way from being palatial, but it was livable, let's put it that way.

But one thing you had to be careful about though, it faced to the south, so, obviously, longways, it was east and west. I was in an upstairs room. And I think the partitions were about five or six feel high. You could look over them to the next one. There was a window on each end of this second story. And you had to be doggone careful that if a guy opened the window on the west end not to open the one on the east end. Because it was just like a wind tunnel. I swear, it would take the sheets right off the beds. So, that was the earliest of what they had—supervised living conditions.

Don mentioned the insect problem when we first came out here, that they had some cockroaches. But we have no mosquitoes out here. We have a mosquito abatement program, and that's kind of a slush fund for people that they want to benefit. Because

The Antelope Valley Fair and Alfalfa Festival reflected the area's rural nature. While it had the displays typical of county fairs — such as farm machinery, livestock, and arts and crafts — it also featured the role of aviation in the area's economy. Here the X-4 and D-558-I were displayed at a fair in the early 1950s. (E-828)

there's nothing for these guys to do at all, as far as I know.

We had no fleas. My daughter lives over in Newport Beach, and she has two cats, and the cats would get fleas. So she would bring them here for a week, then take them back, and they were completely deflea-ed. No problem at all. We have plenty of ants, but we don't have the mosquitoes. Oh, let me tell you how bad it was back at Langley Field. Don knows this. You'd be working up in a wheel well; you were pulling the airplane out, and you had to put the canopy down. You go to hit a mosquito on the back of your head; your head goes back; and you've got a new, fresh-cut in it. Right? We flew into Wallops Island about seven o'clock at night, and I ran into the Operations Room and beat mosquitoes all the way. This is hard to believe, but we had to have the windshield wiper on the station wagon because you couldn't see through the mosquitoes on the windshield. That's a fact. So those are things that we left behind. There was mention, also, that Willow Springs was completely utilized by the Bell Aircraft people, but that was not so. We had Dick Paine in there. Bud Rogers was there. Three or four of them were there, and we would go to Willow Springs, Saturdays and Sundays, and the gals would have a picnic and all that. But there was— The swimming pools were very nice, and—

BORCHERS: Almost lost my son in this big system that they call the swimming pool, about six, eight feet deep. Gilbert Sousa was the mechanic who was to watch my son. My wife come back, and here was my boy down there and I had to dive in and rescue him.

BAILEY: I did the same thing to— You remember Walt Frazier?

BORCHERS: Yeah.

BAILEY: His kid. All these people sitting around this thing. This kid went in and went down underneath and didn't come back up. Nobody paid any attention to him. Like Don says, about six or eight feet. I went down and picked this kid up and held him up over my head, and I didn't think anybody was going to take him out of my hands. It looked like we were going to have to pull him down back up.

Did a lot of hunting. After we came out here a while, I had a lot of applications from people from Langley Field that had heard about this that wanted to come out here. But we were limited as to how many people we could have. So its reputation was not such that these people weren't willing to come on out here or even look at it as a better opportunity than what they had back there at Langley Field.

I noted on here that the erroneous information that was submitted as factual regarding maximum temperatures at Muroc. I believe they said, in 1945, the temperature was 144 degrees out here. I called the library, and they did a research job for me. The maximum temperature ever recorded was 134 degrees, at minus 168 feet sea level, in Death Valley in 1913.

BORCHERS: I might have to disagree with him a little bit. I'd go into the instrument shop, and I'd get a thermometer, and I'd go out and put it on top of my blue Dodge. The thermometer always exploded about 140 degrees.

COX: That blue Dodge kept changing color all the time.

BORCHERS: Borchers. I'll tell you how crazy we were in NACA. In 1950, Walt came to me, and he said that the Fairgrounds wanted to have a couple of airplanes. So I requisitioned a flatbed, and I had a D-558-I and a[n] X-4, brought them in. There was three of us. So, here we had $4-million-worth of airplanes, didn't have anybody in front of us to clear them on the road.

SPARKS: No nothing!

BORCHERS: It was like another day at the races.

BAILEY: We take exception to the statement that our people were frequently drunk here. We never had any problem with alcoholism—at all, that I know of.

BORCHERS: Even at the party times.

BAILEY: No. Mmmm mmmm.

BORCHERS: We were all a bunch of guys—28—20 years old, at the time, having a family and—

COX: Yeah.

BAILEY: We sure don't want a bunch of drunks.

COX: I think that point is certainly valid, and I go back to the business of, it's like a family. I don't think anybody particularly wanted to embarrass themselves in front of the family. We didn't have a bunch of drinkers, anyway, as far as I knew. Unless we got the people from Langley out there.

BORCHERS: Only one time. We were having a party in Clyde's house, and somebody proposed a strip poker game. We started playing, and Joe Vensel got all upset because his wife had to take her top off or something. I went out and challenged everybody that had gone out. But that's the only rowdy thing we ever had.

COX: But it seems to me, when you're dealing with sources, and particularly about something that is in the past some, there's a certain amount of flavoring involved in these things whether it's intentional or not. It just gets that way. Speaking for myself, the older I get, the more those things grow in their intensity.

GORN: Sure.

COX: This has been good for me because it kind of made me stop and think about all the good times.

BORCHERS: They talk about the wind and dust and all that. We would sweep the hangar out, but it wasn't bad.

BAILEY: We did that at Langley.

BORCHERS: I know. Well, I was just watching the new pictures they have at NASA, the films, and they talk about the dust, how we used to sweep the dust off the airplanes and all that. I don't remember any of that stuff.

GORN: One or two people have said something about dust that would come in. In the very early days, that would come in through cracks in the windows and would get into the bed and that kind of stuff.

COX: When my wife and I moved into Lancaster [there] was something less than 4,000 people there. There was no build-up [areas] to the west of us, and I could look as far as across the railroad tracks and as far as I could see, there were very few houses. In fact, there were three houses available when we moved in, and one of them had just recently been built. But the windows were all sash type. They were always a big run on masking tape, because the ladies would seal around the windows. But that's a part of living on the desert. Everybody planted cottonwood trees and elm trees, and so on, because that helped break the wind. Then ten years later or 15 years later, they were sorry because it all got into the sewer system. Mr. Roto Rooter made his retirement, working around here cleaning out the pipes. But, basically, there was a lot of dust blown. The wind blows on the desert.

But, golly, no place you go is going to be perfect by any means. And, so, you— Clyde was talking about—and Don—about the problems back on the East Coast. And we have our earthquakes, and so on, and so forth. A lot of people just say, "I don't see how you can live there in the first place." And then the other people that are saying that cyclones and typhoons and—or whatever—hurricanes.

BORCHERS: Well, I want you to close this thing, Mike, by telling everybody that we think it was the best years of our lives, the beginning of NACA at Muroc.

COX: Amen!

GORN: Well, I think one of the things that we can easily fit in is the sense of camaraderie. What I'm thinking now is, maybe because the camaraderie and the work was so good, maybe, even if conditions were not the greatest sometimes, you'd say, "Well, so what?" You're working long hours with people you like; you're doing work you love.

BORCHERS: Remember, I just came out of the Navy in the South Pacific. And to see the stuff over there, this was luxury.

BAILEY: Well, Don Thompson said the same thing.

SPARKS: I don't think you can go anyplace in the country and have perfect weather.

BAILEY: At Langley, it would snow—on the inside in the wintertime; no place to get warm. And you don't work with gloves on.

COX: There's a compensation. And that's the other part of this. Like I say, you're naive when you believe that any place is going to be perfect, obviously. And the other part of it is that if you're doing something you love, you overcome a lot of other things. Than again, coming from the local area, I had it made in southern California. There were other places I could have gone to work after I got out of school. I chose to come up here, and I chose to stay here.

BAILEY: Speaking of long hours, when I went to work at Langley Field—and this was true all over—we worked five-and-a-half days a week. We got off at noontime if we were lucky. When we got off a noontime, I'll tell you, we swept out the hangar before we left. I had about 15 people working for me and responsible for one hangar there. So, long hours were not anything new. When I came out here, they couldn't pay you overtime, but they would give you comp time. I brought 400 hours out here with me. I had enough time to build a house in Lancaster without taking any annual leave at all.

Have you ever bitched because somebody said, "Well, you're going to have to work until this thing is finished"? Never happen. We spent many a night there, 24 hours a day, that we didn't even go home. Most of our work started at three o'clock in the morning when we were flying the X-15 and the X-1. And everybody that you needed was out there.

GORN: Don Thompson was talking about Ma Greene, who you mentioned. And this is just asking you a question to confirm it-[he] said that you could be working late into the night; someone would call her up and rouse her out of her bed. She'd give him hell, but she'd still open up [her café].

COX: She adopted people. I mean, the guys, the workers. She really did.

BAILEY: I was there one time when Bob Hope came out. He was going to do a thing for the people out there. He stopped at Ma Greene's for breakfast, and I was there. He was real careful to explain to Ma that he wanted his eggs sunnyside up; he didn't want any of them broken. She took the damn egg, did like that; it splattered. She said, "If you can fry them damn eggs without breaking them, come up and get behind the counter." We met a lot of people out here, Hollywood types. All of us worked on pictures at Edwards, the X-15 story and the X-1 and all of those things.

BORCHERS: The story of Pancho using filthy language, I never ran into it when I was there.

BAILEY: As far as Pancho running a "cathouse," that was not the case.

GORN: She wasn't a madam.

BAILEY: No.

BAILEY: The day that the X-1 broke the sound barrier, the 14th of October, [1947] I had go back to Washington, so I wasn't here. That night, Lewis called me, cryptically told me that they had broken the sound barrier. This was not in the newspapers until months later. But, anyway, our two pilots, Herbie Hoover and Howard Lilly were out here. And, of course, Mildred was home alone with our daughter Sandra. Howard and Herbie came over and said, "Mildred, we're going to have a big party out at Pancho's tonight." She said, "Well, I can't go." She said, "I can't go up there alone." They said, "No, if you come with us, we're going to protect you." Mildred said, after about 11 o'clock, she didn't see anything of Howard or Herbie, either one of them.

SPARKS: We always had a first-flight party at Pancho's. Every time we had a new airplane out of Northrop, if we flew it up here, why, we had a party over there. I was kind of used to those things, and I didn't think much of it. But after I went to work for NACA, the first flight on the X-4, John Griffith flew it. Scotty Crossfield would then fly the next one, and he was going to go over there to Pancho's. Walt Williams says, "Well, I'll go, too." Joe Vensel says, "Yeah, I'll go, too." So we all piled into my car and went over to Pancho's. Scotty and Griffith had a little bit too much to drink., and they were picking on Walt. Well, Walt worked them out by the pool, and all of a sudden, he picked both of them up and tossed them into the pool. Now, this was in December. There was no ice on the pool, but I had to bring those guys to town with stinking clothes. I had a new Ford that had a heater in it. So, I went out and got it running and got it warmed up a little. They came out from setting in front of the oven and jumped into the car and off we went. Vensel co-piloted for me.

BORCHERS: I'll tell you a story about Scott [Crossfield] I always tell. We'd just gotten the D-558-II with the rocket in it. And the CG [center of gravity] had changed on it. I found it in the hangar and crew chief Dick Hanna put a 55-pound block of lead right underneath the seat. The thing is, the nose used to come over, and it used to tip out. And I said, "Well, I'm not going to let that airplane fly like that." Scott came around here, and he raised hell with me. He punched me in the chest. "You know what's wrong with this place?" I said no. He said, "Too damn many mechanics playing engineers." I said, "Well, I'm sorry, Scott." He said, "I am going to talk with Walt." And Walt says, "If Borchers says that airplane's not going to fly, it's not going to fly."

Well, he comes huffing back and he goes into the rocket room, and he took a flexible hose and hooked it up to an oxygen tank, turned that sonofabitch on—and it's a hydraulic line—and it just about missed his head—just spun around like that—he came out there white as a sheet. I punched him in the chest. "Too damn many engineers playing mechanics." He didn't talk to me for six months!

COX: You know, though, I had the same experience with him, too after we had had quality operations going. One of the mechanics said he didn't want to let the airplane go. I said, "Okay. Fine." Then Scott came down, and he yelled at me like he yelled at you, and he didn't really punch anybody. He does it to stir the pot, anyway. I think he really was wrong—in my case, at least. So, he finally says, "Damn it, Cox," he said, "it's my life!" And I said, "Damn it, Crossfield, it's our airplane!" And that was the end of it. He just kind of grinned, and he went away.

BAILEY: Joe Walker would get all upset, and he'd call my desk; I'd answer the phone and start saying something. And he was so pumped up, he wouldn't say anything. So if nothing came over, I'd hang the phone up. Then he'd [come] down the stairs and into the office. "You hung that phone up on me!"

BORCHERS: Oh, man, I had one day. Joe had come out, and we got talking. He's from Pennsylvania. He has a farm or something there. And he was talking about a horse and a mare and how you hook the things up. And I was just leading him on. I said, "Joe, you're-out of your damn mind; it goes this way." And everybody knew I was just putting him on, but he was getting hotter and hotter. I never hooked up a team of horses in my life.

BAILEY: He had a short fuse.

COX: Yeah. One of the funniest things, I think, about Joe Vensel— And he was such a sweet guy, a really, really good guy. He lost his hearing flying open-cockpit airplanes. But he had one of the old-fashioned-[hearing aids]....It was a big, big hearing-aid...a big amplifier. And what was the name of the girl that spoke so softly and— His secretary?

BAILEY: Dana?

COX: Yeah, Dana. And she was a little, sweet girl, but she spoke real softly. And she'd go up and talk to the guys, and she was a little bit awed by it. And as she talked, she'd look down. She'd look down like this, you know, And Joe was cranking up the volume. He says, "You know," he says, "there's something wrong." There was nothing wrong with the thing. She just wasn't saying anything. We laughed about that.

BAILEY: By the same token, we would have these long, drawn-out staff meetings, you know? And Joe would get tired of that and turn that thing down.

SPARKS: I think the thing on that staff meeting was the time he'd been away for six weeks or something, came back, and we're having a staff meeting. And didn't do anything that way. Come to find out, he had his hearing fixed. You know, he caught everything we were saying. And, before, unless you talked right to him, he didn't hear you.

BORCHERS: We had a guy named Marion Kent in the procurement section of the base. Norman Hayes and I and he would always flip a coin up against the wall and see who bought the Coke. The odd man bought. So I went into the machine shop, and I made two pennies with double heads. And we got [the Cokes] every day for months and months and months, he never did find out.

GORN: Well, these are all examples of the kind of tapestry you're talking about. Now, when I talked to De Beeler, Mr. Bailey, he said I shouldn't turn off the tape recorder until you tell me a little bit about the P-51 tests.

BAILEY: Well, they were way, way back, when I first went to work there, we put a glove on a B-17 and pumped air through it to get the laminar flow going across it. Then the next project was trying to get free flow. The tunnel couldn't get two-percent flow across it. So we put a small glove on a P-51 and put a [model]. We took an X-1 [model] and sliced it right down through the middle, put it down flat on the wing, and then we got the flow across there. We had a fifty cell manometer in the wing—which was the largest and the only wing we had at the time—and took readings from that. So it gave a pretty good indication of what you could expect. Multiply it by the size of that thing, which was about a one-eighteenth scale model. I think that Bill Gray did most of the flights. Well, on a P-51, if you go for that max speed, you can get control reversal on this thing. Gray was flying it, and I think he started around 10- or 12,000 feet, and dove it to get max [speed] which is probably about 600 miles an hour or in that neighborhood. And he got control reversal. Before he got thing squared away again, he was at about 600 feet from the ground. So the guys stuck their necks out pretty far before we ever had an X-1 airplane.

BORCHERS: Well, we were flying some of them that didn't have a glove on; it just had the manometer on the wing. On the pitot.

BAILEY: But with a glove on it, you wouldn't have to fly the airplane quite that fast in order to get the flow.

BORCHERS: That was something, we used an eighth-inch copper tubing, drilled a hole and ran it all the way into the manometer.

COX: Well, Mike, what kind of additional questions do you have?

GORN: Well, I think you've pretty much stopped me.

From the pages of the X-Press.

> **CLYDE BAILEY TO RECEIVE SERVICE PIN TONIGHT**
>
> At a stag dinner this evening, Clyde G. Bailey, Superintendent of Flight Maintenance, will be presented with his 15 year Meritorious Service Award.
>
> Mr. Bailey joined the NACA at Langley on March 17, 1941, as an Aeronautical Mechanic. He officially transferred to HSFS on August 24, 1947. Last month he was appointed Safety Officer for the Station.
>
> Mr. Bailey makes his home in Lancaster with his wife, Mildred, and their two children.
>
> Fifteen year pins have been previously presented to three members of the HSFS staff—Norman Hayes, Joseph Vensel, and Chief of the Station, Walter C. Williams.

> PROUD PAPAS - Two HSFS'ers were recently added to the list of proud papas: Clyde Bailey (Aircraft Maintenance), a son, Berkley B., who weighed-in at 7 pounds 7 ounces on Thursday, February 7; and Jim Martin (Research Engineering), a daughter, Mary Helen, on Saturday, February 9 at 8:08 p.m. Weight - 7 pounds 13 ounces.

> HSFS'ers do get around...especially Ralph "Sparkie" Sparks who left Friday, August 17 on a flying trip to Panama, with side-trip visits to old friends in Puerto Rico, Venezuela, Nicaragua, and Guatemala. Sparkie will be accompanied on his trip home on September 4 by his daughter who has spent the summer in Balboa, Panama, visiting Sparkie's brother.

JOHN GRIFFITH

Interview by Peter Merlin, February 2, 1998

Left to Right: Bob Champine, John Griffith, and Joe Vensel.

Over the decades, research pilots always held an essential place in the history of the NACA. They collaborated with engineers in all aspects of the experiments. As a result of the increasing complexity of aircraft, more and more research pilots became engineers themselves. John Griffith was an example of this new type of pilot. He showed his flying skills in the South Pacific during World War II. After the war, Griffith earned an engineering degree with honors. He subsequently joined the NACA's Lewis Flight Propulsion Laboratory (now the Glenn Research Center) where he undertook icing research and ramjet tests. Griffith arrived at Muroc in August 1949, and over the following year and a half, flew a wide range of experimental aircraft. Griffith made nine flights in the X-1, three in the X-4, fifteen flights in the D-558-I and nine in the D-558-II. He left the NACA for Chance Vought in 1950, and subsequently worked for United Airlines, Westinghouse, and the Federal Aviation Administration.

Q: If you could possibly tell me a little bit about where you were born, and when you were born — a bit about your background and education.

A: Okay. I was born in the Cook County Hospital in Chicago, Illinois, May 19, 1921. I grew up in Homewood, Illinois. The Depression was pretty tough in those days. My father had a hard time making ends meet, and we lost our home in 1940. But I finished junior college in 1941. I got into the Army Air Corps, and flew 189 missions in P-40s in the beginning of 1942 and '43. When the war was over, I finished up my last two years of engineering at Purdue University in aeronautical engineering, where I graduated with honors in 1948.

Q: What spurred your interest in aviation? How did you decide to become a pilot?

A: Well, when I was growing up in Homewood, airway green three went near our house. I could look up there and see the DC-3 flying along Goshen, and Toledo, and Cleveland to New York, and I thought: Boy, that really must be a great thing to be up there flying that airplane. I read in a magazine about a pilot that went through [pilot training at] Randolph Field and flew P-12s in Panama. Thought that was interesting. So I pretty much had an ambition to be a pilot.

Q: Can you briefly describe your World War II experience — where you served, what airplanes you flew?

A: Well, I went to flying school at Corsicana in Randolph and Foster Field. And then I got flight training in fighters in a P-43 at Spartanburg, in P-40 at Myrtle Beach. I had 45 hours in fighters when I went to New Guinea in September of 1942, and I flew the P-40 there for 189 missions and 450 combat hours.

Q: What can you tell me about icing and power plant research that you did at Lewis Aeronautical Laboratory in the late 1940's?

A: Well, after I graduated from Purdue, the first people that came down to interview me was Ed Gough and a couple other guys from Lewis Lab. After they gave me an offer, I decided that I'd go to work there at the Lewis Lab. The main icing research was done with the B-24, with the J-34 engine mounted under the wing. We flew through icing conditions, and I remember one flight that the ice actually built up on the engine cowls to the point where the propellers were rubbing the ice. In the B-24, the pitot is underneath the airplane, and the ice built out far enough on the mast that even though the head was heated and kept the ice off of that, the ice went around in front of the pitot. We flew the final approach on the ILS with pitch attitude rather than air speed.

Q: Was there any other research piloting that you did at Lewis and at Langley?

A: Well, they had a crash program at Ravenna, that they were going to crash C-46s, and I think it was C-82s, there. I worked out taxiing a C-46 back and forth on the runway the distance it would take to get to 100 miles an hour, and the trim position that you would need for a level condition to go into the crash that they were simulating at Ravenna there. We also did some work with a B-25, and had a Black Widow P-61 there as well. Ed Gough was flying a P-75 with a double Allison engine, but I didn't fly that airplane.

Q: How was your research flying different from the flying you did for the Army Air Forces?

A: Well, in the Army Air Forces, the mission was either to dive bomb, or for intercept bombers, or have aerial combat with Zeros. Whereas in the research, we were out to try to get answers that would enable people to fly in icing conditions. The B-24 had a heated wing that prevented the ice from forming on the wing, and there was de-icing on the propellers. So the airplane was pretty well protected. These were things that eventually came onto the commercial flying that enabled commercial flying to be conducted with icing conditions.

Q: How did you happen to be transferred to Muroc?

A: Well, Mel Gough was Ed's brother, and he was at the Lewis Lab one day. He said it looked like there was going to a requirement for another pilot at the High Speed Flight Research Station. I immediately said that I'd like to be that pilot, and so they evidently gave me the chance.

Q: Well, what did you think when you got there? What were the conditions like?

A: Well, before I went to Muroc, I went to the Langley Lab to do a bunch of dive tests with a P-51. I flew with Herb Hoover, who had flown the X-1, and flew a seaplane to Wallops Island and back a few times. I actually flew a B-29, flew an F-80, F8F, and quite a few different airplanes just to kind of get [experience], even though I had already probably flown most of the World War II fighters. It was with Herb Hoover helping me, and telling me about what the X-1 was like, and things that way. It was good training for going to Edwards and flying the X-1.

Q: What did you think of the facilities when you got there?

A: Well, I guess most people say that they were fairly spartan. There's a lot of wind, and dust, and dirt, and there was just the hangar there. Of course, we all had offices and desks. There was an adequate area where they did the data reduction, and writing the reports, and turning out the technical papers. I thought it was an up-and-coming operation.

Q: Who were some of the people that you worked with then?

A: Well, Walt Williams was running the place, and De Beeler was helping him. We had Sig Sjoberg and Hubert Drake as engineers. Joe Vensel was my immediate boss there, and Bob Champine was already there flying the X-1 when I got there.

Q: Can you characterize the people who made the greatest impression on you?

Ground photo of the Douglas D-558-I Skystreak research aircraft. A Navy-sponsored project, the Skystreak flew at speeds approaching Mach 1. Its jet engine allowed the aircraft to sustain these speeds for prolonged periods, increasing the amount of data collected per flight, and adding immensely to the understanding of the transonic speed range. (E49-0059)

A: Oh, everybody was friendly, and we got along well. I don't think there was any special — I did have quite a bit of respect for Walt Williams. I think he was working quite hard to make the thing go.

Q: What sorts of equipment were available to support the research flying?

A: They had the X-1 and the D-558-I and -II, and the X-4 was coming along later. They had quite a good cadre of people that were working on the instrumentation, and maintaining the airplanes, and all the rest. The oscillograph instrumentation was well developed, and gave pretty good answers, and air speed, and altitude, and control forces, and G forces and all the rest that went on in the airplane. And, of course, on the X-1 we measured pressure distribution over the wing and the loads on the airplane while it was going through the transonic and supersonic speeds. Did rolls and pull-ups and things that way, and up to the indications of what was going on with the airplane during these things. Then, of course, they analyzed the data and wrote the reports.

Q: What sort of aircraft did you get to fly while you were there?

A: Well, other than the X-1 and the D-558 research airplanes, we had an F-84. Then later on we had a P-51, and we flew a C-45 and a DC-3.

Q: Did you have any interesting experiences in some of those?

A: Well, the D-558-II in a pull-up, the down wash from the wing would hit the horizontal tail and cause a sharp pitch up. I had done some lower speed pull-ups, and the pitch up was not too severe. But I think I was about 280 knots or something like that. And on that [faster] pull-up, why when the down wash hit the horizontal tail, the airplane quickly pitched up to a stall and went into a spin, and [I] recovered from that and went on. And on that same flight, they wanted a stall maneuver. It was getting late in the flight, and I was only 14,000 feet. I would have preferred to have done a stall at at least 20,000 with this airplane, since I had never done a complete stall with it before. Sig Sjoberg had said he wanted to get the last gasp of this stall. So I was sitting there at 14,000 feet with the gear and flaps down, and as I slowed down, why I could feel it start loosening up quite a bit. I kept on pulling back on the stick, and suddenly the right wing dropped, and it started yawing off into a spin. I knew that the [spin] recovery was unsatisfactory with gear and flaps down. So I quickly retracted the gear and the flaps,

A Douglas D-558-II Skyrocket taking off from the lakebed. Completely different from the jet-powered, straight winged Skystreak, the Skyrocket featured swept wings and a variety of propulsion systems. Flying a Skyrocket, NACA research pilot Scott Crossfield became the first to fly faster than Mach 2. (E49-219)

The instrumentation carried aboard a D-558-II. The complicated research needed to understand high-speed/high-altitude flight required an extensive package of data recording equipment. After each research flight, this data underwent reduction and analysis. (E52-872)

and I was pretty sure I was going to exceed the speed for those anyway in the recovery. I believe I held the rudder against the yaw. It was the only chance to do a normal spin recovery. The FAA used to say [to] hold it in full controls for two turns in the spin, and then hit the opposite rudder, and pop the stick forward. That was supposed to recover from the spin, but with this airplane, and the altitude I was at, I was sure there was no chance to go through all of that maneuver. I just held the rudder against the yaw, and first thing you know, I had the nose pointed down. I pulled it out and recovered.
I later did an analysis from the telemetering data. I had started at a 14,000 feet, and I recovered at about 7,000 [feet], indicating about 300 or 320 knots. But got it out alright. As I remember, Walt Williams and Joe Vensel were on the lake where I was going to land, and they had some field glasses. I understand that Walt was watching this stall, and when it started to go off into the spin, why he handed the field glasses to Joe Vensel and said, "Here," he says, "you look." But anyway, that was a little excitement on that flight.

The Northrop X-4 on the parking apron. One of several research aircraft built to test different wing configurations at transonic speeds, the X-4 project concentrated on swept wings without horizontal stabilizers. Although this design proved unstable at speeds near Mach 1, the aircraft was useful in such areas as low lift over drag landing training. (E50-360)

Q: Would you describe your fastest flight in the number two X-1.

A: Well, I don't remember whether that was the flight that we did the pull-up or the roll. I got to 1.2 Mach number according to [Richard] Hallion's book. I really think that some of the Mach numbers he's got in that book were not right. I know that there were several of the flights that he mentioned showed .98 or .99, and I'm sure that after the first two or three flights, I was always up to 1.15 or something like that.

But we normally did a roll or a pitch up at the end of the speed run, at the maximum speed we could get when the fuel was getting low and you knew it was going to run out before long. In the pull-up, the controls all were at the transonic and supersonic speed. The cord on all the controls on the X-1 were pretty small, and the pitching rate and the roll rate was much less. But I gave a full aft on the stick, and I probably gave about a half a G. Then I did the stabilizer trim, and as I remember, I got up to almost seven G's before the airplane stalled. But after it stalled, the stabilizer was in a position that wouldn't allow any recovery. So I had to run the stabilizer back to the position that the airplane would fly before I recovered. It was just kind of flopping around in a stalled maneuver.

Q: And while you were out at Muroc, where were you living at that time?

A: We lived at 1012 Date Street here in Lancaster.

Q: Oh, right downtown.

A: Just drove by the house there today. I planted a tree in the front yard. It's a big tree now.

Q: I'll bet it is. I'll bet a lot has changed.

A: Oh, yes.

Q: What were the conditions like then? What was Lancaster like at that time?

A: It was a small town. I don't think more than two or three thousand. Beyond [Avenue] J to the south and 10th Street to the west, there was mostly desert. But there's sure a lot of things here that weren't there in the 1940's. I might mention that a three bedroom house with a detached garage was $11,000. Our principal, interest, taxes and insurance were $69.00 a month.

Q: Wow. So, why did you decide to leave the NACA?

A: Well, in the fall of 1950, they were going to do this movie "Jet Pilot." There were people up there that were painting the airplane for the movie. They started talking about their salaries, for some reason or other, while I was sitting there. I thought: These guys painting this airplane are making more money than I am. It was just a few days after that that J.R. Clark, Chief Engineer from Chance Vought came by, and offered me this job flying the [F7U] Cutlass at Dallas, at Hensley Field, and the opportunity to almost double my salary, and with the bonus program, maybe three or four times the salary I was making. So I was influenced by the money, and left the NACA.

Q: Can you describe your test piloting after you left?

A: Well, I was Senior Experimental Pilot on the F7U, and I had some pretty exciting experiences with that airplane. The first six F7Us that were built — the three X's and the first three production F7U-1s — five crashed and three guys were killed in it. I had a wife and three little kids, and I thought: Oh, I think I'd like to see these kids graduate from high school. So after a year with Chance Vought, I went with United Airlines.

Q: You worked for United Airlines?

A: Yes. I initially went to work for United in 1952 from January until April. In April I went to work for Westinghouse as a Chief Engineering Pilot for their Gas Turbine Division. But I worked for them for eight years, and they went out of the gas turbine business. Then I worked for FAA from 1960 until 1966. United was hiring flight instructors, so I put in an application. And they hired me in April 1966. I flew on the airline out of Chicago for about seven years, from 1970 until 1977. Then I went back to Denver as a flight instructor. At age 60, why it was mandatory retirement. So in 1981, I was retired as a flight instructor.

Q: What are the flying achievements that you would say you're most proud of?

A: Oh, I've pretty well probably covered flying the X-1 and the D-558s. The X-4 I had more publicity than any of the rest of it. They put my picture in the Los Angeles Times. Marvin Miles wrote an article on it. Well, I just enjoyed all of the flying I did, and I was glad that I was a pilot and had the career in aviation.

There are some regrets that I have — that I made honor grades at Purdue in aeronautical engineering. I feel like when I was with NACA I should have gotten into the report writing, and more into the technical aerodynamics, etc. that was going on there. I probably wasted a fair amount of my time between flights, when I could have been doing work with Sig Sjoberg and Hubert Drake. I really wish I had gotten more into the technical part of it. I didn't, and so hindsight is good.

But, I do really feel very fortunate to have survived my aviation career. I think that probably a third of the pilots in my flying school class didn't make it through World War II, and three of the pilots before me in the F7U were killed. I had a fair number of close calls, and I really feel very fortunate to have gotten this far.

Q: Are there any other achievements in your life that stand out in your mind particularly — anything that you're proud of besides flying?

A: I did quite a bit of work in the Little League in the time when my kids were growing up. Cub Scouts and Boy Scouts — things that way.

Q: Do you have any observations to add other than what I've already asked you about?

A: Well, one thing about the flying that was done at Edwards AFB. I was wondering why as many guys went as high as they did and lost control of the airplanes. It would seem to me that somewhere along the way they would have put a little more effort into stability augmentation, or some type of thrusters, or something like that that you could mount on the airplane, and approach these speeds and altitudes in smaller increments. Milburn Apt goes up on his first [X-2] flight and die because he really didn't have the experience of approaching the problems in a slower and easier manner.

Q: Yes. They pretty much had him bite off the whole thing at once with the flight to Mach 3.

A: Right. He was the fastest man for a little while, but not very long.

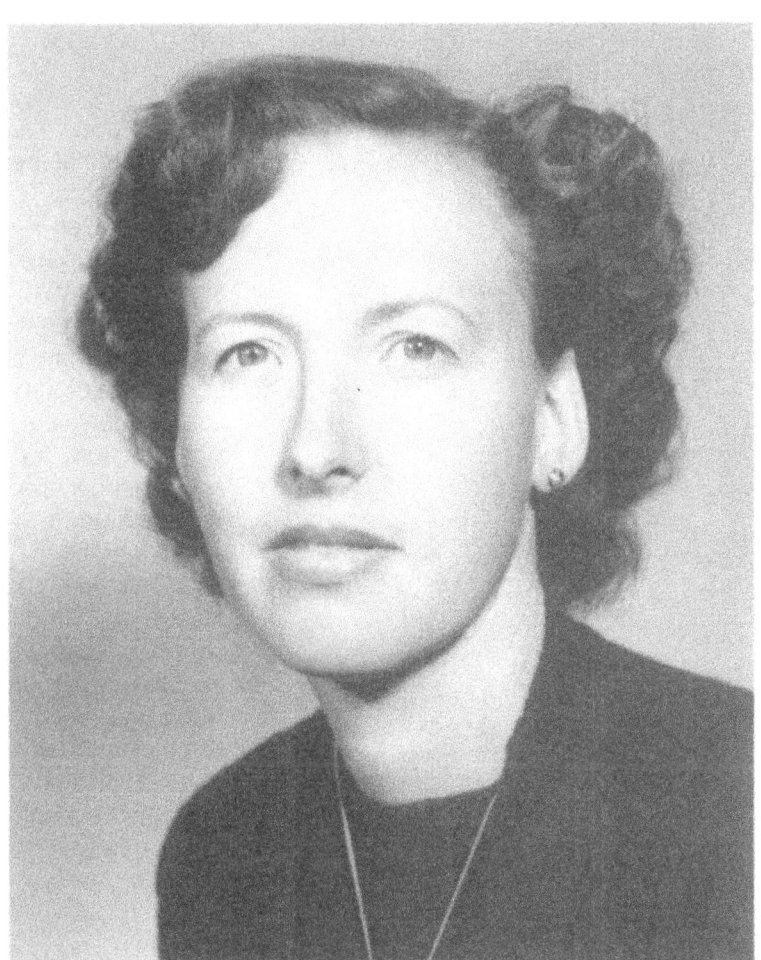

BETTY LOVE

Autobiographical sketch June 2002

Betty Love started work at the NACA as a "computer" in 1952, several years after the initial influx of Muroc employees. Two "computers" — Roxanah Yancey and Isabell Martin — had been part of the initial group who joined Walt Williams when the NACA facility opened in late 1946. During the 1940s and early 1950s, the term computer referred to a human (usually female) who performed the calculations to convert instrument readings into engineering data such as altitude, true airspeed, Mach number, and control positions. Like the male employees, their numbers rose as the data processing demands increased. Three NACA computers worked at Muroc in October 1947. By the end of 1948, the number had grown to eight. Even so, when Beverly Swanson (Cothren) arrived in 1949, so much backlogged data existed that she worked weekends for the first month and a half on the job. Like the male employees, the computers had to deal with acute housing problems. Between December 1946 to the spring of 1949, Yancey moved from Kerosene Flats, to the hospital area housing, to the Air Force nurse's quarters, and finally, to the NACA Women's Dorm, where she spent five years. The different social environment of a half century ago resulted in a high turnover among the computers: some left due to the harsh conditions, others got married and quit when they had children, some left when their husbands transferred or found new jobs. The computers held a unique position in the history of aeronautics. Their work -

The entrance to the NACA Women's Dorm at South Base. To improve the housing accommodations on Muroc, new men's and women's dorms were completed in the spring of 1949. The Women's Dorm had ten single rooms that rented for $6.92 biweekly. This included maid service and use of a washer and dryer. A new computer received a salary of less than $100 every two weeks. Each room also had its own evaporative cooler, but separate kitchen and shower facilities.
(E96 43403-8)

conducted in a man's world of engineering — determined the overall quality of the research of their day. Betty Love's story illustrates not only her own life, but life in her era.

The side and parking area of the Women's Dorm. These vehicles carried employees around the NACA facilities, and on trips to and from Los Angeles. Located down the flight line from the NACA hanger, the Women's Dorm stood near the base cafeteria, theater, and chapel. In contrast, the Men's Dorm on North Base was some eight miles away. Its distance required the Men's Dorm to have its own cook and kitchen. (E96 43403-7)

I was born in Pasadena, California and moved to the Antelope Valley in 1930 when I was eight years old. The family consisted of a stay at home mom, a father who was a finished carpenter and a younger sister. Dad built our home on 40 acres of farmland on Avenue F, 1/4 mile west of 50th Street East. I graduated from Antelope Valley High School in 1939. During those school years I had decided I wanted to be an airline hostess. One of the requirements was to be a RN [registered nurse]. I attended Antelope Valley Junior College taking science courses and some math so that upon graduation I would be able to continue in the Nurses Program at Los Angeles General Hospital. At the time that was one of the best nursing schools. Upon graduation in 1941 with an AA with a science background. I was accepted into the nursing program for September 1941.

Well needless to say plans changed. I married, moved from the Valley, my husband at that time was working for Lockheed in the experimental shops as a jig and fixture builder. I raised two children, My husband and I returned to the valley after being gone four years. I wasn't employed, but became President for the PTA and did all the 'mom' things of those days. Both children were in school and we had friends that had coaxed my husband into going to work for NACA at South Base in 1951. The next year the friend said, "Betty they need computers, I think you would qualify why don't you apply" so in January 1952 I went to work for NACA as a computer. The pay was great, I was all of a GS 1. It was several years before my two-week paycheck would equal $100.00.

Working as a computer one would reduce the data from research flights and by calculations convert the inches of deflection on a record (film) to engineering units. I was never told what we were actually doing or how it associated with the X-planes. Any one with any idea of math could have followed the instructions of: read the record with a six-inch scale and write it in column 1. Add or subtract a given correction that

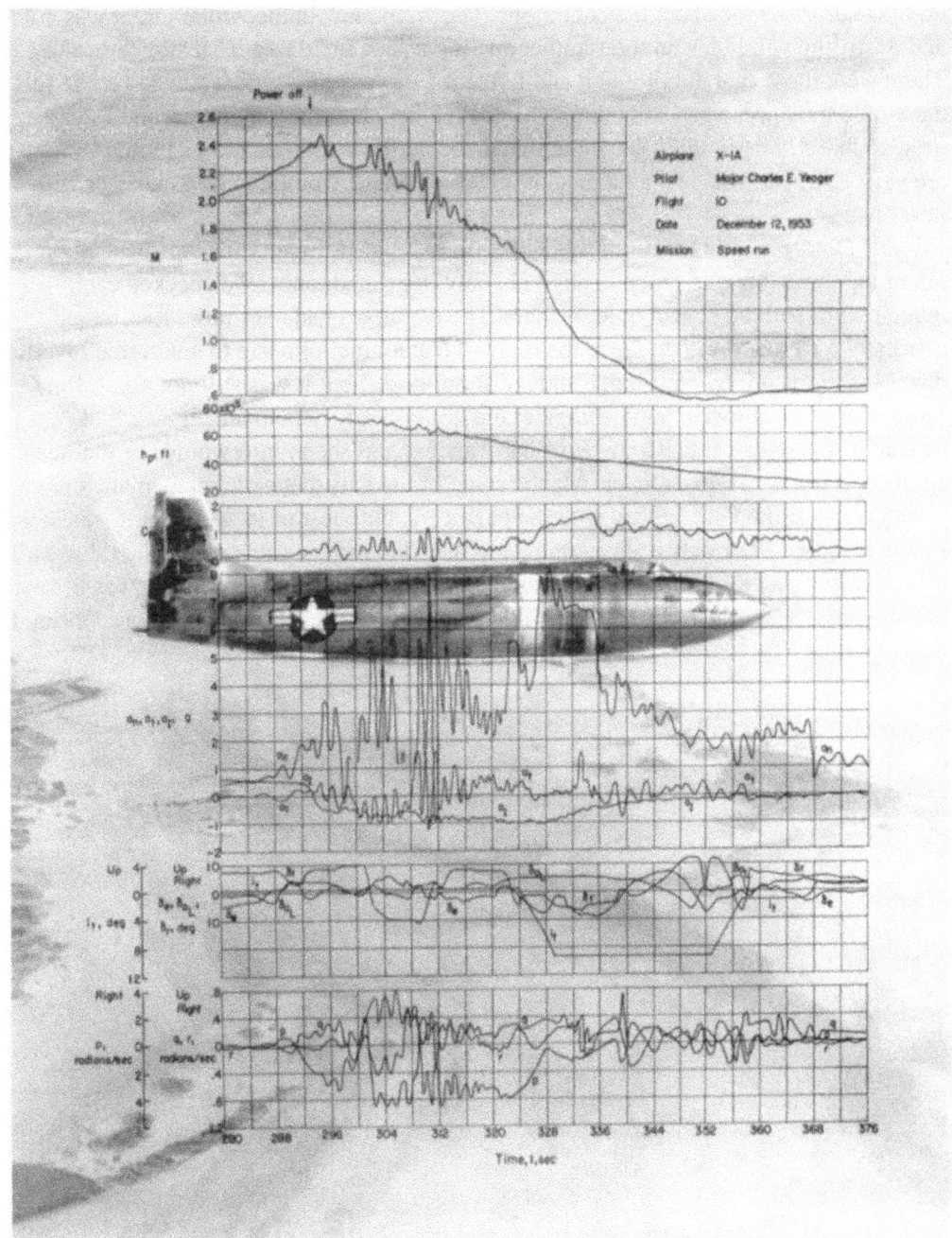

Instrument measurements from Maj. Charles E. Yeager's Mach 2.44 flight in the X-1A on December 12, 1953. The X-1A encountered instability, and tumbled completely out of control. The X-1A fell for about 50,000 feet, entering an inverted spin. Yeager recovered into an upright spin, regaining level flight at low altitude, and finally glided to a landing on Rogers Dry Lakebed. Betty Love and some of the other computers reduced the data for this flight. Among the data shown are Mach number and altitude (the two top graphs). The speed and altitude changes due to the tumble are visible as jagged lines. The third graph from the bottom shows the G-forces on the airplane. During the tumble, the aircraft twice reached 8 Gs, or 8 times the normal pull of gravity at sea level. (E-24911)

came from pre and post flight calibrations and write in column 2. Take that figure and go to a calibration chart for that airplane and flight and write that reading in column 3. This would be the final engineering unit if it were an acceleration or a roll or angle-of attack record. If it were airspeed-altitude record you would continue by calculated the columns as the heading directed or looked up numbers to use from tables. Also, if one paid attention to what the trace was doing, going up or down, then when the calculations were finished you could scan the sheet and tell if you had a wrong reading. Not at first, but after a short time one could do this.

The computer room was at the end of a series of huts all strung together. Right next to my desk was a steel rod that ran from floor to ceiling across and along the near wall. There was a long hall way with the engineering offices on either side. This unit was attached to the main hangar, the only hangar, where the coffee was, by an enclosed breezeway. Further on down the hall and towards the front of the building were Walt Williams' and De Beelers' offices and a secretary. The administration and financial people were in another building just a short ways away. I had lived in the valley, so nothing surprised me about the conditions. The wind blew in the winter and it was cold and dusty, the wind blew in the summer and it was hot and dusty. That was the valley. There were those that didn't like it and left and there were those that stayed for the job, but would move on when something else looked better. Some just stayed and I guess grew to like it. I lived in Littlerock at this time and the weather patterns in this valley are very different from one area to another. Much later I would live in Lancaster with a new husband.

The atmosphere in the room was like a library except for all the Friden calculators humming away. No one spoke to any one, only in hushed tones. We checked each other's work and did so in a quiet manner. The engineers had a lot more fun in their offices. We were allowed to leave the room two at a time for a trip to get coffee twice a day. Most of us brought our lunch and ate at our desks, but it was still not noisy. Rest room trips were allowed, but a computer did not take any data to an engineer but instead it was returned to Roxie [Roxanah Yancey] and she in turn would see that the engineer request was given back. Maybe some of the gals that were mathematicians were given a little more leeway with the engineers, but most of us were not. I was lucky in lots of ways. After only a short time I was asked to print some large posters. I wasn't told what for, just the words that would go on them. Later I found out there was to be a meeting and these signs were placed on the displays. Don't ask me how I was chosen, I don't know.

The computer's office at South Base, circa April 1949. In the left foreground is a Friden calculator. The individuals are, left side, front to back, Mary (Tut) Hedgepeth, John Mayer, and Emily Stephens. On the right, front to back are, Lilly Ann Bajus, Roxanah Yancey, Gertrude (Trudy) Valentine [behind Yancey], and Ilene Alexander. The computers worked under strict supervision. When an X-plane landed, they could open the window blinds to watch, but could not go outside, as this violated the rule prohibiting long breaks.
(E49-0054)

There was one lady, Joan Childs (Dahlen) that was an engineer when I came to work. She was a computer and had the same restrictions. There were times when she stretched those, but I guess, she knew how far she could go. After we moved to the new building [in June 1954] there were several lady engineers, Harriet Smith being one of the first. I respected those ladies and knew that their chosen profession wasn't all smooth sailing. In some ways I had more leeway than they did. Here again I was never sure why.

Later, I noticed that I was getting data to reduce with special instructions. Rather than read the trace from a reference line in the normal manner, I would read the amplitude of the trace or the width. Later [I would] count the frequency of certain peaks that exceeded a measurement. It wasn't long until I was working with the engineer. In 1954, after our move to the new facility, I was removed from the computer office and placed in with four engineers that were doing structures work. Buffet, vibration and flutter. One of those engineers was the one I had been working for earlier. I still had my Friden [calculator] and still did the same data reduction, but just for the office. Also I could ask what was I doing, what was it going to be used for, and I did ask lots of 'why' questions. All were answered and lots of times I was shown the airplane and the parts we were looking at. I said, I was lucky.

The computers did not just work hard under strict rules. Following a snowstorm in late 1948, a group of them pose with a snowman. Back row, left to right, are: Mary (Tut) Hedgepeth, Lilly Ann Bajus, Roxanah Yancey, Emily Stephens, Jane Collons, Leona Corbett, and Angel Dunn. In the front row, kneeling left to right are: Dorothy Crawford Roth, Dorothy Cliff Hughes, and Gertrude (Trudy) Wilken Valentine. On the right edge of the picture, looking out an emergency exit, is Walter Williams. (E49-0212)

I don't remember ever asking about a raise, but they came at regular intervals right up until I retired. I was given a new title with the move. Aeronautical research engineering technician.

While working with the structures group I kept receiving more responsibility always with instructions and a gentle push along with, "You can do it". If there wasn't enough work to keep me busy I was farmed out. To aid other engineers with their project, to the flight operations branch to type transcriptions of the flights, to do drawings, make films, I was always busy and enjoyed what ever I was doing. I enjoyed working and learning from everyone. I worked on all the research airplanes from the X-1 and the D-558-II to the X-15 and the XB-70. Monitoring the flights to listen for the reports of the pilots of what they heard or felt from the aircraft. Noting times so I could correlate it with the flight records later to find the problem.

Later when the telereaders came along I would read data [by putting crosshairs on the trace and pushing a foot peddle] and punch the data into cards rather than writing it in columns. Then take the cards to the card sorter and do statistical work in that fashion. I was working on the X-5 at this time. I was taught how to punch cards by hand, how to write a short program to reduce the data from cards. It was done on the new big frame [electronic] computers.

Another fun program was when Mr. Beeler asked me to work with Mr. [Tom] Fisken the illustrator on a movie. Mr. Fisken wrote some of the shows for TV, Bonanza was his big one. He knew all about storyboards and timing a film and I got to look for the film footage that he needed. We timed it, found the original film and made trips to Lookout Mountain [Air Force Station] in Hollywood to process the film. A professional narrated the film, "Pathway to the Stars." It was about a day with Joe Walker, pilot, in a flight of the X-15. Another time I edited and produced a silent movie that ran in a continuous loop for a display in Washington D.C. on all of the X Planes; the X-1, D-558-II, X-3, X-4, X-5, X-15.

In seemed like the engineers were always looking for a dimension on a plane or a photo for their reports. Seeing a need for a storybook, I put together for each plane we were flying a table of dimensions, a three view drawing, around the clock photos and whatever else I found of interest during the search. Those books were used by anyone needing the information.

I was given the first programmable desk computer. That was fun to learn and I reduced data for several engineers. It used punched cards or preprogrammed data in cards.

I was co-author on some publications, third author on others. I located the required data to be presented, reduced, plotted the data and would do the figures for the reports. I was given permission to do a buffet boundary once on the X-3. When the boss came back, he checked it and said, he couldn't do better and told me he knew I could. I was afraid I would make a mistake that would cause trouble during a flight. Today I find my name referenced in new reports and some of the data that I had been asked to compile being used. Makes me feel a little special. Another project was to keep a flight log of the research flights. Dates, pilot, and what was accomplished on the flight. Any pertinent information to that flight.

As far as advancement. Like I said before my boss gave me lots of encouragement to go as far as I could with the education I had. I did return to the Antelope Valley College and take two math classes, but without a degree I couldn't go too far and I had attained that goal. I was pleased and satisfied with my duties. I never felt I was restrained in any way. I know the gals weren't allowed in the hangars to work on the planes, but I felt free to go most anywhere and did with work orders and instructions for a project to get on the road. I knew most everyone. I started in January 1952 and I worked until June of 1973. My husband, Jim was ready for retirement, so I was told that my position was going to be abolished and that I could return to data systems when a position became available. I wasn't thrilled at that prospect, so when the age factor and the years added up for retirement I retired.

There never was a dress code. The women worked in the offices and dressed accordingly. Skirts and blouses, suits, pretty shoes and hair always just so. That was the period in time where that was expected. The fellows wore clothes appropriate to their job. Engineers were usually in slacks, white shirts and ties, with a jacket always available to slip into when required to go to the front office or when company arrived. The flight operations fellows (there were no girls), wore coveralls, nice work pants (no Levi's) or on hot days one would find them shirtless, but no shorts. As I said, that was the dress for everyone whether they worked at NACA/NASA or the Air Force, or anywhere else.

It used to be there was a code of bells for the management. One for Williams, two short ones for Mr. Beeler and so on. The Branch chiefs had one bell with a space and then one or two bells however they were assigned. Now we have this public address system that calls out names and numbers all day long. Also, it used to be that the chief or director circulated among the employees. Always interested in what was going on. Played cards during lunch with the various card-playing groups. They knew their employees. Now that doesn't happen. Could be because of other demands, I don't know. [Paul] Bikle [the director after Williams left in 1959] was always playing games with the crews, whether they be mechanics or engineers, betting them they couldn't get two successful flights on two different X-15's in the same day. More or less challenging everyone to do better, but I'm sure the safety factor was always in place.

I believe that when Williams or Bikle was the director, they were here to see that research was done, and took pride in what they did. Some [later] directors, were here for the experience to get to the next rung on the ladder.

I found that the whole process was enjoyable and challenging especially when you knew what you were doing and why. I've tried to think of a time when I didn't want to go to work or was not ready when the bell rang at four o'clock. The car pool used to give me fits, because I was the last to get there and they were in a hurry to get home. That was, until Neil Armstrong joined the car pool, then they left me alone and got all over him for not being ready at four o'clock. I just enjoyed doing what I thought was expected of me. Some of the people I had on pedestals.

OPENINGS FOR MATH AIDS ANNOUNCED

Immediate openings at HSFS for Mathematics Aids, GS-2 through GS-4, were announced today. Salaries range from $2960 to $3415 per annum.

The Mathematics Aid, GS-2 must have one year experience or have successfully completed a full four-year or senior high school course which has included two one-year courses in mathematics (algebra, geometry, or trigonometry). Full-time study successfully completed in a resident school above high school level may be substituted year for year for the required experience up to a maximum of four years provided this study has included or been supplemented by six semester hours in college mathematics in such courses as algebra, trigonometry, analytic geometry, and calculus for each year of education substituted. These positions are limited to women only.

Employees who know qualified persons who are interested in these positions are asked to contact the Personnel Office.

From the pages of the X-Press.

Section II

A Second Wind

The move to the new NACA facility at the Edwards Main Base in 1954 not only reflected a recognition of the permanence of NACA flight research at Edwards, but also a shift in the research emphasis. The High-Speed Flight Station no longer existed solely to fly faster. Both military necessity and research imperatives still pressed researchers toward higher Mach numbers, but subjects such as high speed stability and control now became critical as well. Aircraft design underwent fundamental changes as a consequence of supersonic flight. To reduce drag at high speeds, aircraft now had shorter wings, while fuselages became larger and heavier to accommodate jet engines and their large fuel supply. The North American Aviation F-100A embodied this new structure. Called the "Super Saber," the F-100 represented the first U.S. production aircraft capable of reaching Mach 1 in level flight. This feat constituted a great performance improvement over the F-86, then the standard Air Force fighter. But the new aircraft designs, with their mass concentrated in the fuselages, began to encounter compressibility, turbulent flow, and shock patterns that resulted in reduced stability. Indeed, routine operations at supersonic speeds constituted an unknown territory, and dangers awaited both the experienced test pilot and the inexperienced second lieutenant.

Inertial coupling represented one such danger. This problem only became a serious one with the development of post-war jet fighters. Under specific flight conditions, the distribution of their mass, as well as their heavy fuselages caused movement in two axes (roll and pitch) to result in an uncommanded movement in the third axes (yaw). The possibility of inertial coupling in aircraft had first been identified theoretically as early as 1948, and remained a potential problem for another six years.

Then, in 1954, several F-100As broke up in flight. In one instance, North American's chief test pilot, George Welch (former Army Air Corps pilot and a hero of

Completion of the new buildings for the High-Speed Flight Station in 1954 signaled a number of changes for the NACA group at Edwards AFB. It marked the shift from the makeshift wartime facilities at South Base to a permanent presence. The new building represented an expanded research capability, required for the new challenges aeronautics faced in the mid-1950s. (E54-1254)

Pearl Harbor), made a rolling pullout over Edwards, only to have his F-100 yawed more than 15 degrees to one side and disintegrated. There had been warnings of problems before the crashes. Lt. Col. Pete Everest, an Air Force F-100 project pilot, had argued that the aircraft needed to be modified to correct poor supersonic directional stability, but U.S. Air Force Headquarters overruled him, and the F-100A entered production. With the fleet grounded, and hundreds of F-100s on order, the Air Force needed a quick fix, and turned to the NACA for help.

Gen. Albert Boyd asked Walt Williams to assist with the effort. NACA engineers knew something about inertial coupling. During a supersonic flight, the X-3 experienced violent roll, pitch, and yaw motions. It had reached its maximum load limit, but both aircraft and pilot survived. As a consequence, the High-Speed Flight Station began an intensive series of stability tests with the F-100, resulting in an unofficial program between the Air Force and the NACA to evaluate a range of military aircraft such as the F-102, F-104, F-105, and JF-107A. The NACA's research into inertial coupling discovered both the cause and the solutions. Even so, inertial coupling still posed a threat to aircraft and pilots. In September 1956, the X-2 went down on its Mach 3 flight due to inertial coupling. Even with such aircraft as the X-15 and the space shuttle inertial coupling remains a concern.

Stability problems did not just concern inertial coupling, however. The new swept and delta wing designs — especially during low-speed/high angle of attack flight or in high-g turns - sometimes fell prey to "pitch up." This phenomenon occurred because the downwash from the wings struck the horizontal stabilizer, forcing the airplane's nose upwards. The search for an answer to the pitch up tendency resulted in extensive testing of different designs of chord extensions and wing fences, and finally required changes in the horizontal stabilizer position. These and other improvements characterized the second phase of flight research by the NACA at Edwards AFB, discussed in the following pages.

SQUARE DANCE SCHEDULED FOR APRIL

The annual Station Square Dance has been set for Friday, April 22, at Juanita's Indian Lodge in Rosamond, Activities Committee Chairman Vernon Dore announced this week.

According to Mr. Dore, Herb Perry widely known square dance caller, will be on hand to "call" and to lend a helping hand (and foot) to the not-so-expert "dos-a-dosers".

Dancing will begin at 9 p.m. highlighted by an 11:30 p.m. buffet supper of assorted salads, turkey, seafood, and ham. "Juke box" music will be furnished for interim popular dancing.

Appropriate dress for the evening will be Levis for fellows and ginghams for gals.

Tickets, $1.75 per person, may be obtained from Activities Committee Representatives and entitle the holder to a chance at three door prizes. (Ticket holders must attend the dance to participate in the door prize drawing.)

SOFTBALL

A practice of the NACA softball team will be held on Saturday afternoon, June 25, from 2:30 to 4:30 in Jane Reynold's Park.

The opening League game is, at present, tentatively set for sometime within next two weeks. When available, definite opening date and game schedule will be posted on Station bulletin boards.

In a recent practice game with Convair the NACA players came out on top with a 10-2 score.

Team co-captains, Ed Holleman and Joe Walker, report positions are still open and urge all interested persons to attend the June 25th practice.

FIRST ANNIVERSARY PARTY TO BE HELD IN JUNE

Preliminary arrangements have been completed for the June 25th First Anniversary Party, for all NACA employees and their guests, Activities Chairman Vernon Dore announced today. The party marks the completion of one year of occupancy of the present Station facility. A dance and a buffet supper will be featured.

Music for dancing beginning at 9 p.m. will be furnished by Paul Blakely's seven-piece orchestra. The buffet supper, prepared under the supervision of Al Hauser, will be served at 11:30 p.m. Bar facilities, handled by the NCO Club, will be set up in the cafeteria.

Tickets, including the supper and dancing, are $2.25 per person and entitle the holder to participate in door prize drawings. First prize will be a $25.00 Savings Bond.

Tickets may be purchased now from Activities Committee members.

OPERATION OF DORMITORIES TO BE DISCONTINUED

Operation of both the men's and women's NACA dormitories will be discontinued no later than April 30, 1956. This action has been considered necessary since the original purpose for which the Station assumed operation of the dormitories (to provide batchelor type housing where none was otherwise available) is now being fulfilled by housing developments in Edwards and surrounding communities.

In addition, effective December 1, 1955, rental rates for the dormitories were substantially increased. All present dormitory residents have been notified of the increase.

From the pages of the X-Press.

NACA EXCHANGE SPONSORS RAFFLE FOR CRUSADE FOR FREEDOM DRIVE

The annual fund drive of the Crusade for Freedom will be highlighted this year, according to drive chairman Phil Walker, by a raffle of a 3-speed Decca record player.

Chances on the record player will be sold at $1.00 each by section attendance clerks. Mr. Walker pointed out, however, that the raffle must be cancelled unless a minimum of 150 chances are sold.

The Crusade for Freedom is a movement to enlist the support of Americans in an effort to carry the truth behind the Iron Curtain and to give new hope to enslaved people. The principal weapon of this crusade is Radio Free Europe, which reaches 70,000,000 people in the captive countries of Poland, Czechoslovakia, Hungary, Romania and Bulgaria.

RFE has exposed Red collaborators. It has undermined Red regimes. It has given back to the people their culture suppressed by communism.

The HSFS campaign for Crusade for Freedom contributions begins today, Mr. Walker stated, and will continue throughout next week.

TENPIN TALK

At HSFS NEWS deadline, Schizofrantics continue to lead the current NACA Mixed Bowling League with 32 wins and 24 losses. Following in second position are Brown & Co. with 28 1/2 wins and 27 1/2 losses. Individual averages are:

STANDINGS

Team	W	L	Avg.
Schizofrantics	32	24	
Harriet DeVries			127
Ernie Cadle			156
Don Reisert			107
Beverly Russell			114
Brown & Co.	28 1/2	27 1/2	
Allen Brown			148
Paula Truesdell			94
Dale Reed			119
Terry Larson			151
Cotton Pickers	28	28	
Dan Riegert			151
Peg Sutphin			94
Don Hallberg			121
Joe Babine			129
Three Hits & A Mrs.	23 1/2	32 1/2	
Norman Musialowski			137
Pat Musialowski			102
Harry Curley			136
Rex Cook			107

EMPLOYEES CAUTIONED TO OBSERVE BASE SPEED LIMIT

All HSFS drivers are cautioned to carefully observe the 35 mile per hour speed limit maintained within the Base proper. Infraction of the speed law may result in removal of a Base decal for a period of two weeks, or more.

LOST

"Welding Handbook" by American Welding Society. Last seen in X1-E parts cabinet during week of March 1, 1955. Please return to Kenny Kleinknecht.

From the pages of the X-Press.

POLIO IMMUNIZATION SET FOR MONDAY

First, second, and third polio shots will again be offered at no cost to employees and their families, it was announced this week. On Monday, January 13, from 2:30 to 5:30 p.m. the vaccinations will be given in the Main Base cafeteria. The cafeteria is located on the corner of Mojave Boulevard and Wolfe Avenue, diagonally across from the Civilian Personnel Office.

It will be the responsibility of individual employees to make arrangements for their families. Shots will be administered to infants 6 months or older and to adults under 40 years of age.

Employees, with the permission of their supervisors, may be excused from work for the time required to receive the shot.

DATE CHANGED FOR CHILDREN'S CHRISTMAS PARTY

Attention: Santa's Helpers

Santa Claus will be at the Park View Cafetorium on Friday, December 20, at 7 p.m., instead of Wednesday, December 18 as originally scheduled. According to chairman Dick Cox, the Party committee (composed of personnel from the Operations Division) has been diligently working on pre-party arrangements. Approximately 175 children of HSFS'ers are expected to be greeted by Santa. The program has been planned to be entertaining and not lengthy, Dick says, so all can be home and tucked in by the usual bedtime.

From the pages of the X-Press.

HIGH ALTITUDE RESEARCH PROGRAM PROVES VALUABLE

Initial data about gust-meteorological conditions to be found at 10-mile-high altitudes which have been obtained to date by the relatively few flights of Lockheed U-2 airplanes have already proved the value of the aircraft for this purpose, Dr. Hugh L. Dryden, NACA Director, said recently in a national news release.

"The airplane has shown its capability to climb 50,000 feet and maintain that altitude for the time necessary to obtain the research information desired," Dr. Dryden said. "Further, it has adequate load capacity to accommodate the data-gathering instrumentation required."

Research flights covering the western part of the United States are being made from Watertown Strip, Nevada. Within recent weeks, preliminary data-gathering flights have been made from an Air Force base at Lakenheath, England, where the Air Weather Service of the USAF is providing logistical and technical support. As the program continues, flights will be made in other parts of the world.

The instrumentation carried by the U-2 airplane includes special equipment furnished by the Wright Air Development Center and the NACA.

(Reprinted from "Wing Tips")

BIRTHS

TIPTON - a daughter, Patricia, born Thursday, March 10, to Mr. and Mrs. Joseph Tipton (Aircraft Maintenance), 7 pounds 10 ounces.

VEITH - a daughter, Sheryl Ann, born Tuesday, March 15 in Lancaster to Mr. and Mrs. Robert Veith (Aircraft Maintenance), 5 pounds 14 ounces.

RED CROSS DRIVE COMPLETED

A total of $59.40 was collected in the Red Cross Membership and Fund-Raising Campaign conducted throughout the Station during March.

WANTED - Used typewriter. Contact Joe Lattanzi at Ext. 45 between 3:30 and 4 p.m. or at 28771 (Men's Dorm) from 10 a.m. to 3 p.m.

WANTED - Plate glass mirror, approximately 3' x 2'. Contact Harriet DeVries, Ext. 13 or Johnnye Green, Ext. 23.

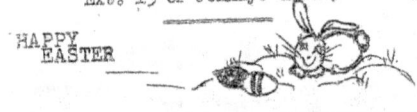
HAPPY EASTER

EMPLOYEES URGED TO CONTRIBUTE TO HUNGARIAN RELIEF

In response to an emergency appeal for funds, contributions for Hungarian Relief are now being accepted by Dorothy Fleming, room 112, Personnel Office.

The urgent appeal for $5,000,000 to assist the Hungarian people in their hour of need has been launched by the American National Red Cross, under the personal leadership of President Eisenhower.

In a letter from Chairman Philip Young of the Civil Service Commission, the support of all Federal personnel was solicited. Mr. Young stated, in part, "All Federal Service military and civilian personnel in all parts of the world are urged to respond generously to this emergency appeal. Local chapters throughout the country and overseas representatives of the American National Red Cross have been advised of the urgent need for prompt action. The heads of all Federal establishments and installations at home and abroad are urged to cooperate fully in this first emergency appeal under the fund-raising policy and program for "true voluntary giving" approved by the President on June 27, 1956."

LANGLEY SCIENTIST ORIGINATES SUB-SATELLITE

Some of the earth satellites which will be fired hundreds of miles high as a part of the research programs of the International Geophysical Year will carry "sub-satellites", it was revealed recently. The sub-satellite will be made from aluminum coated plastic, and will be automatically inflated after it has been ejected from the third rocket booster that sends the satellite itself to its maximum altitude.

William J. O'Sullivan, Jr., aeronautical research scientist at Langley Laboratory, is credited with having conceived the novel manner of construction. The sub-satellite will be inflated to a diameter of 20 inches, the same as the satellite itself. Including the necessary inflation gear and container, the sub-satellite will weigh only 10 1/2 ounces. Larger sub-satellites, which may be built for later uses, would be visible to the human eye.

RICHARD E. DAY

Interview by Dr. J. D. Hunley, May 1, 1997

Richard E. Day began his career at the High-Speed Flight Research Station in 1951, initially on the X-1 and XF-92A aircraft. He was then assigned to support the Air Force on the X-2 flight tests in 1953. During this period, Day programmed an Air Force analog computer with the X-2's flight characteristics. Operating this primitive machine — the first rudimentary flight simulator — he predicted the aircraft's stability at higher speeds and altitudes. Day became involved with inertial coupling in 1954, following the loss of two F-100s and a near accident in the X-3. Understanding the reasons for inertial coupling required Day and the engineers at the High-Speed Flight Station to apply theoretical studies to the real world flight conditions. Stability calculations had long been done for aircraft, but to solve the problem of inertial coupling required a fundamental change in procedures. Analog computers were used to simulate the inertial conditions which led to the crashes. The switch from human to analog (and eventually digital) computers had a profound impact on aeronautical engineering. The analog computers may have been slow and limited in their capability to model an aircraft's stability, but they were quickly adopted not only for research proposes, but also for data analysis, simulations, and pilot training.

Q: First of all, I wanted to ask you about your date and place of birth and a little bit about your family background and your education if you wouldn't mind.

A: Okay. I was born in 1917 in a little town in Indiana, Windfall, Indiana. It was named because a tornado had destroyed it at one time. I graduated from high school there. Then after high school I had two years of college at Indiana University, and then I dropped out to do some work. In 1938 I got my pilot's license and [two years later] went to Canada to join the Royal Canadian Air Force as a pilot. Is there anything particular about education?

Q: Did you finish up at Indiana University?

A: Oh, yes. With a Bachelor's degree majoring in physics and math. I started in graduate work. And at that time I decided I really wanted to go to work. So I applied to NACA.

Q: Right. Now, you say you came to Dryden in 1951?

A: Yeah, on Labor Day.

Q: I read your paper on inertial coupling, I don't have a copy of the draft, so I don't have perfect recall of everything you discuss in there. But, as I recall, you discussed the technical issues very thoroughly, but I don't remember that you talked very much about the design changes that resulted from the findings about coupling phenomena. So I wonder if you could comment about some of the specific design changes for future airplanes that resulted from the coupling work that was done on the X-2 and the X-3 and so forth.

A: Well, that coupling came about primarily because of inertial properties and poor directional or longitudinal stability. If an airplane rolled at the same frequency as the stability, well, then you'd have a resonant coupling. Now, there are several things that can fix that. One of them is good damping, which you didn't have at high altitude and high speed, but they put automatic dampers in before they had the complex computer systems to control them like they have today.

Q: These were dampers on the pilot's control stick?

The sleek looking Douglas X-3 lacked adequate propulsion from its twin jet engines. Intended to reach speeds of Mach 2, it barely exceed Mach 1. The X-3's long fuselage and low aspect ratio wings, however, made it an ideal vehicle for inertial coupling research. (E55-1996)

A: Yeah. Well, the dampers were mainly on the rudder. Say, as if you'd have yawing angular velocity, the angular velocity would feed into the rudder and damp it. And damping's an angular velocity sort of thing. That cut down on coupling. And then, later on, as the computers came in, you had powerful actuators, big control surfaces, and, stability-wise, you could fly a bowling ball. With all the computers and control surfaces from that point on inertial coupling didn't become a problem. So the improvements that took care of the inertial coupling were the control systems we have today that take care of any type of instability, and powerful actuators, that is, to boot the control surfaces, and make the control surfaces larger so they could get out of these coupling problems. So the main thing was the computer and better control surfaces which overcame the coupling.

Q: All right. Now, you mention [William H.] Bill Phillips' theoretical discovery of coupling phenomenon ahead of the actual experience, and you even blame him for it occurring, facetiously. How much did his theoretical work help out in the actual flight research that you were doing in the work with simulators?

A: It was almost essential. It was great, because nobody had any idea what had happened, and until they read Bill's old 1948 report, just purely theoretical, only a few people in history had done that, like Newton or Einstein's theoretical predictions and it happens. So once the F-100 and X-3 got into roll coupling, somebody either at Edwards or back at Langley said Bill Phillips has written a theoretical report on this. So Walt Williams sent Hubert Drake and Joe Weil back to Langley to talk to Phillips, and they had put this on their analog simulator. However, they didn't have pilot control. It was automatic input, program input. So they learned all they could from Bill and those people and came back. Then the Air Force had bought this GEDA (Goodyear Electronic Differential Analyzer), an analog computer. Joe Weil and I went over there and we programmed it or mechanized it, as they called it, with five degrees of freedom. And we used that from then on. That was absolutely essential. Phillips' document [Effect of Steady Rolling on Longitudinal and Directional Stability (NACA TN 627, 1948)], and the analog computer, just essential in solving the problem.

Q: I want to ask you about the simulator and also about Joe Weil in a little bit. But first, I think, just to follow up logically on something you said a moment ago and is in this Air Force interview: You mentioned the fact that when the roll frequency and the pitch or yaw frequency were resonant or the same, that you got into this coupling phenomenon. But could you explain that a little bit?

A: Well, on an airplane if you put a rudder pulse in and stop it, it has sinusoidal, or fishtailing, motion, and the frequency would be so many cycles per second. That's the frequency I'm talking about. It's the stability frequency of the airplane.

Q: But it is a wave?

A: Sinusoidal wave, that type of thing.

Q: It's an aerodynamic phenomenon?

A: Yeah. And it occurs in almost everything, automobiles. But it has quite a bit to do with civil engineering or the structures of a building. Say [in] downtown LA, if this building had a period or cycle, [of] one cycle per second in a strong wind. You had an earthquake occur at the same cycle, one cycle per second, that would be resonance, and knock the building down. But if it were not the same frequency, if it were higher frequency or lower frequency, it would not resonate. So that's what they were trying to get rid of in buildings and airplanes and so forth.

Q: There was a famous incident with a bridge, I believe.

A: Yeah. I've got it on tape in there. The Tacoma Narrows Bridge at Tacoma, Washington — It's remarkable. That thing just whipped around just like that and that was a resonance frequency.

Q: That was the one that Theodore von Karman wrote about.

A: Yeah. And he didn't solve it, he just told them what really happened.

Q: You mentioned both Joe Weil, who I guess was your supervisor much of the time you were here, and Hubert Drake, who became - maybe was at that time, assistant director of research under De E. Beeler, wasn't he?

A: Yes. De was the first director of research, and when he left Joe Weil took over. Drake was one of the smartest men I have ever met. Anything that would come up,

Drake would know about it. He told me about black holes many years ago, 40 or so, and it wasn't very well known. Any new thing that came along, Drake knew what it was. So between him and Joe Weil, they taught me what I knew, and I'm quite grateful to them.

Q: Did either of them work very much on the coupling phenomenon?

A: Joe Weil did. Joe and I both went down to the Air Force on this analog computer and set it up, and we both worked with the airplanes, the X-3 and the F-100. And in addition to that we did a survey of coupling of airplanes, [a] big, thick report. Joe and I wrote that, and at that time Joe did most of the analytical work, and I did the piloting of the thing, and gradually I got into the theoretical part of it.

> NACA PAPERS PRESENTED AT SYMPOSIUM
>
> On February 29 and March 1, 1956, a Roll-Coupling Symposium will be held at Wright-Patterson Air Force Base, Ohio sponsored by the Air Force. A paper by Joseph Weil and Richard Day will be presented by Mr. Weil. Other NACA papers will be given by Stanley Schmidt of Ames, and Leonard Sternfield of Langley.
>
> From the pages of the X-Press.

Q: And your physics, I presume, served you well in that regard.

A: Yeah. I always thought physics was perhaps better than having an aeronautical degree, because besides aeronautics, you could go into all aspects of it. This inertial roll coupling came from physics.

Q: Couple of other questions about people before we go on with the simulator. You worked under Walt Williams both at Dryden and later at Johnson Space Center?

A: Yeah.

Q: And you worked while Paul Bikle was the director for a while before you left for Johnson in '62, I guess it was. I wondered if you would comment on both of those men and their management styles and how they both worked in terms of how their management styles worked in terms of ...the way that the station operated?

A: Well, Walt was a boss-type manager. I mean he just insisted on people carrying out what he wanted to do, and they usually did or else. And besides that, he let his engineers do their work on their own, more or less, just didn't bother us. So that way we had a lot of freedom to do as we pleased, until we did something wrong. Bikle was also the boss type. By that I mean they insisted on work being done and being done on time, so forth. Bikle didn't have much to do with Headquarters. They were supposed to have a headquarters meeting back at Langley once a month or back in Washington. Bikle seldom went at all. He would manage a lot of the program in such a way that he would come in under cost or at cost. But anyway, he was very economical.

Q: Were there any other individuals that were at Muroc or whatever we should call it, since it had different names at different times while you were there, whom you would like to talk about, comment about? Any others that stand out in your mind as having made outstanding contributions.

A: Yeah. I worked for Jack Fischel for a while. He was the branch chief He retired many years ago. I learned quite a bit from Jack. He was a fundamentalist. He always preached the fundamentals, which is a good thing to do in sports and everything else.

Q: I wanted to ask you a couple more questions about things we've already brought up, or you already brought up. One, you mentioned the F-100s, and I know the solution to some of the problems with the early F-100s was to lengthen and enlarge the tail, the vertical tail. Now, did that have anything to do with roll coupling, or was that a separate problem?

A: That was because of roll coupling; the bigger the vertical tail, the more stable the airplane is. That increases the stability, which increases the frequency and damping. So after we went through the flight test, we took flight test data and put it on the analog simulator and found that the damping would pretty much solve the problem.

So North American was to put on a larger tail — they had three of them — in three increments. Well, they had the normal tail, then they had two larger tails, each being larger, A, B and C, they called it. So Tail C, I think, increased the tail area by almost 50 percent. This was in my report.

Okay. So this was the solution. Also, they were going to extend the wing tips to increase the rolling moment of inertia and also the aspect ratio. But anyway, the main thing was the tail. North American was to have that finished and put on within 90 days. Well, the problem was so bad that these F-100s were just having trouble out in the field. They finally had to stop and quit flying them. So North American then put that tail on in nine days instead of 90, and they flew it, found out that was the solution, and then they made up kits for all the F-100As in service, and there was never any more problem with roll coupling. Anyway, Phillips' study was flight-test augmented and with analog studies, gave that solution, and it was truly a solution and it worked.

Q: And you would call that damping, to have a larger tail?

A: Yes.

Q: And the damping worked on the frequency.

A: Yeah. It increases the frequency.

Q: Now, the simulator that you mentioned that you and Joe Weil programmed with five degrees of freedom, you say in the Air Force interview here that that really was the first simulator?

A: Yeah. I put a lot of qualifiers in front of it. There had been simulators. Well, 50 years ago there was one built, but those were made primarily with servos. You could

In-flight photo of the Bell X-2 research aircraft. Built as a follow-on to the X-1, it tested swept wings at speeds of Mach 3. The program suffered delays, in part due to engine problems and the loss of one aircraft during a captive test. Despite its problems, the X-2 set a world altitude record of 126,200 feet. As the deadline approached to turn the X-2 over to the NACA for further research, the Air Force planned a final flight to reach Mach 3. The pilot, Capt. Milburn Apt, had never flown the X-2 before, but did fly inertial coupling tests in the F-100. The flight, made on September 27, 1956, ended in a crash in which Apt perished. (E-6909)

> "THANKS" FROM COL. EVEREST
>
> A letter recently received by Station Chief W. C. Williams, from Lt. Col. Frank K. Everest, Jr., USAF, who left July 22 to attend the Armed Forces Staff College in Norfolk, Virginia, stated in part, "...I wish to thank you and your people for the gift that was presented to me, but most of all, I feel as if I am in debt to you and all the fine people that work there, for the years of fine cooperation and understanding that without, we in the Air Force could have accomplished only a small percentage of the successful flight testing and resulting prestige that we presently enjoy. NACA at Edwards could have, many times, made it quite difficult for us to continue but, the generosity and aid unselfishly given by your people made our job 100% easier and I will always have a warm place in my heart for the NACA High Speed Facility. I'm not speaking only of the X-2 project, although I owe special thanks to Jack Russell, Dick Day, and all those other wonderful guys who worked many long hours without compensation just for my benefit, but of all projects such as the F-100 series wherein your engineers gave us a clear understanding of all problems involved thus preventing possible loss of airplanes and lives..."

From the pages of the X-Press.

put a navigation track on an X-Y plotter and drive the cockpit flight instruments. These simulators were primarily navigational and blind-flying trainers. They weren't adaptable for research purposes where you could go in and change the airplane characteristics electrically. So this was the very first one where we did flight research, got data from flight, that is an airplane — a pilot would do a pulse and we'd get the record back and we'd do a match of that on the analog and get the derivatives (characteristics).

And we also used it as a pilot trainer. I spent a lot of time with Capt. [Milburn G.] Mel Apt and Lt. Col. Pete Everest before their flight in the X-2. And [Capt. Iven C.] Kincheloe, have you heard of Kincheloe?

Q: Yeah. I've heard of Kincheloe.

A: He was four-star material if there ever was one. But anyway, he did the altitude flight on the X-2. And in those three flights, Pete Everest's flight, Kincheloe's flight and the one that Apt got killed in, I wrote a report, TMX 137 covering the three flights. So did I answer that question?

Q: Yes, I think you did. I have a follow-on: Do you know if the people who designed the later simulators profited from the work that you did on the X-2 simulator?

A: I know North American did, because the X-15 simulator was still an analog, it wasn't digital. But it was six degrees of freedom, which was forward. See, we always held speed constant, but when you brought in the forward speed, boy, that made the problem ten times more difficult. But North American Aviation built the X-15 six-degrees-of-freedom simulator. I think they learned a lot from what we did on the X-2. At this same time all the big companies, Lockheed and Boeing and all the other companies were building simulators. Now, I don't know whether they got anything from what

The wreckage of the X-2 following its crash. Captain Apt flew the mission as planned, although the engine burned 15 seconds longer than expected. As a result, the X-2 reached a speed of Mach 3.2. Within seconds, Apt turned back toward the lakebed, and the aircraft fell victim to inertial coupling. It rolled to the left uncontrollably, and the sideslip increased. The rolling motion in the supersonic spin became violent, subjecting Apt to about +6 Gs. Then, within a second, the spin became inverted, and the G forces went from about +6 to -6 Gs, causing Apt to be thrown around violently inside the cockpit. The negative G forces slowly decreased, and he attempted standard spin recovery maneuvers, which were unsuccessful. Apt then jettisoned the escape capsule, the drogue chute opened, and he attempted to climb out of the capsule. Apt lacked sufficient altitude, however, and he died on impact. (E56-2685)

X-2 CRASHES

On Thursday, September 27, the Bell X-2 research airplane crashed into the Mojave desert about 20 miles east of Edwards Air Force Base.

The pilot of the swept-wing rocket airplane, Air Force Captain Milburn G. Apt, was killed in the crash.

A board, composed of personnel from the Air Force, Bell Aircraft Corporation and Curtiss-Wright Corporation, and the NACA, was appointed to investigate the accident.

The X-2, which was to have been turned over to HSFS for testing upon completion of the Air Force program, was the second and last X-2 produced by Bell. The first was lost in 1953.

From the pages of the X-Press.

we did or not, but once you get into it, it doesn't take a rocket scientist to make this into a good pilot simulator, research simulator. So it's just like many things, once the technology's there, just a bunch of interest in all industries; and Air Force and government took it up and developed it.

Somebody told me, and I don't [know who, that] NACA suggested that the Air Force buy this analog computer, and for what reason, I don't know. But anyway, they didn't have flight engineers down there to make the analog computer into a flight simulator. They had electronic technicians who could only set it up for acceptance of the equations of motion of flight. So it wasn't until Joe and I went down there that they set up an airplane on it with five degrees of freedom. An airplane can go forward and backward, that's one degree. Go up and down, that's two. Sideways, that's three. You also have angular freedom, one, two, three. That's six degrees of freedom. We held the forward speed degree of freedom constant. So it was five degrees of freedom we put into it. The five degrees of freedom are pitch, roll and yaw angular acceleration and forward angle-of-attack side slip, that is side motion, and increased angle of attack. That is the body line with respect to the relative wind. So P-dot is rolling acceleration. Q-dot is pitch acceleration, R-dot is yaw acceleration. What a computer does is it integrates the acceleration to give an angular velocity, and it integrates the angular velocity to give it position. So you can pick off any of these quantities to feed back into other parts of the equation. I don't know what else to say about that.

Q: I think we've gotten through the questions I had on the simulator. Now, I take it that most of your work at the High-Speed Flight Station was with dynamic stability and analysis. But were there other areas in which you worked as well before you left in 1962?

A: Well, most of it was stability and control. You know, we did some space work. First of all, the Center used the GEDA we were talking about, to simulate reaction controls on a nominal airplane to determine what the rocket forces should be to give good handling

An early analog computer used to predict aircraft stability and control behavior. This machine represented a major breakthrough, as it enabled the research pilot to gain experience on the ground, and gave advance warning of dangerous flight conditions. Day recalled later that the computer predictions of the X-2's behavior at Mach 3 exactly matched the actual flight characteristics from Apt's flight. (E57-2946)

quality. And what it turned out to be is a certain acceleration in pitch, yaw and roll. So some of the people at Edwards and I helped, but I wasn't the main one; we did determine the handling qualities for a reaction control system.

Q: Now, was this done before the X-1B did its little bit of flight research or after?

A: I'm not sure, because I wasn't the main investigator, but probably about the same time.

Q: I know that they did do a little bit of reaction control work on the X-1B, but the airplane developed some cracks in the LOX tank, and they had to stop, and then they did some work with the F-104 before they actually installed it on the X-15 and did the reaction control [tests] with that.

A: Yeah. I think their best work was on the F-104.

Q: Now you indicated that you were GS-14 when you left the Flight Research Center, as it was called by 1962. Do you mind saying what your grade was when you arrived at Muroc?

A: Oh, that was a GS-5, at $3,100 per year.

Q: So were you on an accelerated promotion schedule from the GS-5?

A: Normally, if you didn't get in trouble, you went from a [GS-] 5 to a 7 to a 9 to an 11 and then to 12, 13, 14 and so forth. So I got them all when I should. You know, in six months you get this, and I had gotten up to the 14 in the prescribed time, that is if you didn't screw up somewhere along the line. I guess I was what you call branch chief at the time and Walt wanted me to go down to Houston.

Q: I forgot about asking you about early housing when you came to Muroc in 1951.

A: Well, we had been in the Air Force for many years and had some pretty weird housing. But anyway, when we got to Edwards they assigned us the officers' quarters on the [Marine] air base at Mojave, and these were small apartments all in line like military apartments are, and they were quite sufficient, the stove and all that sort of thing. However, the wind was something new to us, and the dust storms. The children would wake up in the morning and raise their heads, and there would be a white spot outlined by the dust that had blown in through the cracks. So in the desert you get used to this. But anyway, the housing, to us, was okay, because we had never lived in palaces before.

Q: How many bedrooms did you have in the housing you had?

A: I think at that time we only had one. This was rather small. I expect it was 500 square feet, or something like that. Had a bedroom and a front room, which was kitchen and everything else, and the bathroom, the three rooms.

Q: Did you have any children at that point?

A: Yes. We had two, a 3 [years old] and a 7 [years old].

Q: Now, how long did you stay at the [Marine] housing before you moved?

A: Not very long. We were there, I believe, six months, and we had the opportunity to buy a new house in Lancaster at the exorbitant price of $7,850. It was a two-bedroom, kitchen, bath, living room. This was a very nice house, then from there, why, it wasn't quite as bad as the early days.

Q: You were able, obviously, to afford the payments on that with your $3,000 plus dollars.

A: Yeah, I think it was all of $50 a month in payments.

A. SCOTT CROSSFIELD

Interview by Peter Merlin, February 3, 1998

The ground-based analysis of inertial coupling represented only a step in correcting its ill-effects. Once the problem underwent analysis and project personnel formulated a solution, it still had to be tested in flight. This became the role of NACA research pilot Scott Crossfield. He flew the F-100A inertial coupling tests between October and December 1954 to define the coupling boundary of the aircraft. The risks of these flights manifested itself during an abrupt aileron roll at Mach 0.7 in a short tail F-100A. The aircraft reached a -4.4 g load and a sideslip angle of 26 degrees. Walt Williams observed that a sideslip of this magnitude occurring at supersonic speed would probably have destroyed the aircraft. Of course, inertial coupling constituted only a part of Scott Crossfield's career with the NACA. He made ten rocket flights in the X-1 #2, fifty-three rocket flights in the D-558-II #2 (NACA 144) and eighteen rocket/jet flights in the D-558 #3 (NACA 145). He flew twelve flights aboard NACA 145 using only jet power. Crossfield also piloted the X-4, the X-5, and the XF-92 research aircraft. In 1955, he left the NACA to join North American Aviation, where he contributed to the X-15's design, and made ten test flights as the contractor pilot.

Q: Okay, Mr. Crossfield. If you could just give me a little background. Tell me where you were born, when you were born, and a little bit about your education.

A: Well, I was born in Berkeley, California in 1921, October 2nd. Raised in southern California until 1935. Then moved to the state of Washington with my family who, as a result of the Depression, went to the farm. Raised as a farm boy until graduating from high school in '39. Soloed in 1936. Got my license in 1941 with the — whatever that pilot program was at that time. I can't think of the name of it. I went to the University of Washington in 1941. And in the end of '41 when the war started, I joined the Navy. I was a Navy fighter and gunnery instructor and a fighter pilot for the four years of the war. Returned to the University of Washington after that. Got a B.S. Degree in 1949, and a Master's Degree in 1950, and joined NACA at that time as an Aeronautical Research Pilot.

Q: How did you become interested in aviation? What were your inspirations?

A: My generation was interested in aviation. That was it. As computers are today, aviation was in those days. I first flew in an airplane the year that Lindbergh flew the

Atlantic. I was a model airplane builder. In fact, I held several records of model airplanes, and just kept very active in model building until I went to college. In fact, I developed one of the first radio controlled airplanes back in those days.

Q: How did you come to be a test pilot at the NACA High Speed Flight Station at Muroc?

A: Well, that's kind of a lengthy thing. I stayed at the University. Because at that time, in 1949, I could make more money working at the University as a part time student as I could going out and getting into a job as an engineer. I was trying to negotiate with Boeing to get a job to go back to flying, mainly because there just wasn't really any money in engineering at that time. I was already raising a family after the war. And through a set of very fortuitous circumstances, I got to Edwards before the other applicants for a job that Bob Champine had vacated. So he had done me a great favor by deciding he wanted to go back to Virginia. John Griffith and Walt Williams hired me. And from then on, I think probably the records are there or here at Edwards.

Q: What can you tell me about Walt Williams who was Head of the High Speed Flight Station at that time?

A: Walt Williams is the most unheralded hero of our move into high speed aeronautics and space that there ever was in the world. There has not been, since World War II, a manned advance in aeronautics and space that Walt Williams hasn't been the primary decision maker on go/no go on the things. Of course we know his record at Edwards. And he brought the crew out here, and developed the research airplane programs all through to the point that we now have at Dryden Center.

Williams went to Mercury, and he literally saved it from a national disaster. He was involved in Gemini. And he was certainly involved deeply in Apollo. He certainly was involved deeply in the situation with the [shuttle] tiles, and the operational decisions on the space shuttle. I think probably no man in history, any several men in history, have contributed as much to our ability to go to the Moon and everything else as Walt Williams, in an operational sense. For some reason or other, he never was given the recognition I felt he should.

Q: What was his style of management like?

A: Walt Williams was a Louisiana boy. He was brusk. He had his own opinions. But he reserved arguing. Walt Williams was an ideal boss for me as a pilot. Because he always gave me the prerogative to question what we were going to do on the next flight. And either I had to come up with a reason why, or fly it. Or else they'd get somebody else to do it. But he always gave me that latitude and room to maneuver in. So I never really had to do anything that I was uncomfortable with, flying for Walt Williams. He wasn't a pilot, but he understood pilots.

Q: And at the time you were there, John Griffith was the Chief Pilot?

A: I guess you'd call him the Chief Pilot. He was the only one here when I got here. Bob Champine was the Senior Pilot, and he had gone back to Virginia. John was here, and he wasn't my boss, but he was my mentor, let me put it that way. Because he had been here, and he taught me the way around the system. At that time it was a very small organization — probably 60 or 70 people total, including the janitors — and an old hangar and some Butler buildings on the South Base. So it was a small, tight organization — very productive.

Q: What can you tell me about Joe Vensel, who was the Chief of Flight Operations?

A: Joe Vensel was an old NACA pilot. Had a remarkable record. He also was an ex-Navy man. He was deaf as a post — had sinus problems, and he was a good boss. He defended and kept his pilots going pretty well. If I ever had any criticism of Joe Vensel, it would only be that I thought he was super cautious. I understand he didn't have the "gung ho" attitude, because he was more mature.

Q: So what were some of the first aircraft you flew for NACA?

A: Oh, they had a C-45, and then I checked out in the YF-84. Then I flew the D-558-I and then the X-1 — probably in that order, and all within a few months of getting here.

Q: And what sort of work did you do with the X-4?

A: Oh, the X-4 was a whole buildup of stability and handling, stability and control, and handling qualities of a tailless airplane. With the X-4, we pretty much found out why we may not have solved the problem. They were having the troubles with the Chance Vought Cutlass [F7U], and they [the British] had one Swallow crash that killed Geoffrey deHavilland. The X-4 was a very productive program. We did a lot of things with the X-4 that weren't only involved in it's being a tailless airplane. It was a good test bed for other purposes, as we did thickened trailing edges on the X-4. We did variable Lift over Drag (L over D) landings from probably an L over D of two to an L over D of nine with the airplane, which gave us good insight into pilots preferences, which were useful in coming up with new airplanes like the X-15 and some of the other low L over D airplanes [like] the lifting bodies. But the X-4 was a very good research airplane, for purposes of looking into a tailless configuration, and for other reasons.

Q: Now it seems like a lot of your first flights in different aircraft were a little exciting. Can you tell me a little bit about your first flight in the D-558-II?

The X-4 undergoing maintenance in the South Base hangar. The X-4 was one of the smallest manned research aircraft ever built, but its design allowed easy access to its engines and internal systems. Scott Crossfield flew thirty-three of the sixty X-4 flights made by NACA pilots. (E-1000A)

A: The first air launch in a D-558-II was with the jet and rocket combination airplane. And on that flight I lost the [jet] engine at altitude, and the windshields iced over. I had no instruments, no electrical power. And that was due to a problem we had with a reverse current relay that would not cut in the battery, even thought the engine had spooled down to where the generator was putting out a very low voltage. So an iced over windshield and no radio for a period of time. So all I could do was put the Sun in one place on that windshield and pray that I was right-side up. I could just see a bright spot where the sun was. Then John Conrad, who was with the Air Force as our chase, got on my wing. By then I managed to get the radio going on the battery, everything else shut down. He flew me home, and landed me on the lakebed. Yes. That was an interesting flight.

The D-558-I on the lakebed at the High-Speed Flight Research Station. Crossfield made the first of his fourteen D-558-I flights on November 27, 1950, and flew the last on June 10, 1953. The Skystreak was the workhorse of early transonic research, due to its ability to cruise at speeds close to Mach 1 for prolonged periods. (E-226)

Q: I seem to recall that on your first X-1 flight, the X-1 dropped out of the carrier aircraft and went inverted. Is that right?

A: Well, I launched into a spin. It was kind of a ludicrous kind of thing. The only engineer was setting the stabilizer. He was putting the level on it, and putting the level on the wing. I said, "How do you remember plus and minus signs in doing this?" Because I had worked in the wind tunnel for years where we were always making errors — plus and minus. A minus angle of attack on the stabilizer is a plus in the airplane equations. He looked at me and he said, "What the hell do you know about it, you dumb pilot?" Well anyway, he had set it one degree stabilizer nose down or airplane pitch up rather than one degree up.

So on this, my first launch, I launched out of the B-29, and it immediately pitched up and went into a spin. Pete Everest was chase, and he thought that was kind of a unique way to launch. But the X-1 was a very good flying airplane. And even that heavy, I managed to recover right away, and then went on with the rest of the flight — lit the engines. Did what we were going to do.

Q: I read that on approach to landing, the windshield iced up.

A: That was probably not on that flight. On one of the X-1 flights, Jack Ridley was chasing, and when you came back down, there was a lot of outside air was ingested in the cockpit. That moisture often would ice up the windshield. So on that day, I was turning final to land, and I was blind as a bat. I told Jack Ridley, "Hey. You've got to help me land. I can't see what I'm doing." He just laughed, and said, "Yeah — That happened to me last week."

But I was wearing loafers, and I got my shoe off, and used one of my socks to wipe a hole in the windshield so I could see the flare to land. That was not comical at the time. I had a little bit of a problem. I couldn't get out of the cockpit, because my foot froze to the rudder bar. Clyde Bailey came up, and I told him what the problem was. So he put his hands down on the rudder bar between my foot. His hand warmed it up, and I could get off of it.

Q: Could you tell me a little bit about your work with the X-5?

A: The X-5 — I don't remember how many times I flew the airplane. [Ten flights between 1952 and 1954.] But Walker did most of the work on the X-5. We just did handling quality, stability and control, analysis maneuvers over the speed range and over the wing sweep range. The X-5 was not a comfortable airplane to fly. It had a low-slung engine. So there was a misalignment of the drag axis, and the principal axis, and the thrust axis, and all of that. So it could get into some interesting maneuvers and motions, and that sort of thing. And it was a terrible airplane in a spin. It took a long time to get that airplane out of a spin. Walker and I found out that it took about 10,000 feet. As it turned out, [Maj. Ray] Popson got into a spin lower than that and he went in with one of the X-5's. But it was an airplane that served it's purpose though. It was unique aerodynamically. So it couldn't be used generically. When the wing swept, the tips no longer were the same, and a lot of things like that.

The Bell X-5 on the South Base ramp in 1952, with its slats, flaps, and speed brakes open, and with its wings at a 20 degree sweep angle. The aircraft served as a technology demonstrator for a variable sweep wing system. Although this particular wing system proved impractical, the F-111, F-14, and B-1 all successfully used variable sweep wings. Crossfield flew the X-5 ten times, out of a total of 122 NACA research flights. (E-661)

Q: And could you tell me a little about your first flight in the XF-92A?

A: That was another first flight. And it wasn't really a flight. Everest was going to fly it. Pretty high winds came up. And for some reason or other, he decided he didn't want to fly it. So we were meeting in Walt Williams office. And he said, "Scott, you're going to fly it next flight. Why don't you go out and taxi it home, make a lift off, and that sort of thing." So I said, "Hey, I'd like to do that." Nobody wanted to fly the XF-92. There was no lineup of pilots for that airplane. It was a miserable flying beast. But anyway, so I made the liftoff. He told me, "Keep the nose up so it will slow down. Because it will roll a long ways." Well, I let the nose come down and on the nose wheel. I couldn't get it back up. It didn't have enough tail power to do it. So that airplane was rolling like mad towards the edge of the lakebed. So I was getting ready to pull the gear handle and the fire extinguisher just as I hit the bluff. There was about a three foot rise at the edge of the lake — when I saw a county road off to the left. And I managed to get that thing turned and head up that country road. Burned out the brakes. Just melted them right there. Rolled up that county road about 100 yards. And fortunately no damage to the airplane. Came out pretty well, except the brakes were all burned out. I knew the tires were going to blow. I was sitting in the cockpit. When they went off, I jumped two feet — each one of them — even though I knew it was coming.

The XF-92A undergoing check outs in the South Base hangar. The aircraft, built as a prototype of a delta wing interceptor, never entered production. Once the Air Force test program ended, the NACA took possession of it for a brief period. Crossfield made all 25 NACA flights, between April and October 1953. The aircraft proved instrumental in the adoption of delta wings on the F-102, F-106, B-58, and Space Shuttle. (E52-0697)

Q: Yes. I've seen a picture of that one sitting on the road there. I was trying to figure out which road that was. I haven't found that yet.

A: You know where the Navajo trail was on the lakebed? It was a runway that was laid out to do the Navajo program in those days.

Q: Okay. I know where that is — on the south end.

A: Well, it's kind of at the west end of the Navajo trail. It's just a dirt county road going up there. About a week later, somebody put a sign up there — Crossfield Pike.

Q: That's great. Tell me a little bit about your first flight in the F-100. That was on September 8, 1954 — the famous hangar wall incident.

A: Well, we had just instrumented a small tail F-100 for the purposes of looking into what was then an unknown problem that had been trapping pilots. It was going into a divergent maneuver that was breaking up the airplanes. We got this one bailed from North American to us. We had just instrumented it. On the first flight, I was supposed to have radar. But the radar guys weren't cranked up. So I went out anyway. What the heck — it was just another Air Force fighter. I got up to altitude, and was just going through the familiarity maneuvers. And I got a compressor forward sectional fire warning light. Well, we all knew that probably if you saw a fire warning light and it was true, you should have blown up by then. Because all the accessories were mounted on the center of the engine.

Well anyway, I believed the light. So I idled the engine, and it flickered out. Then it came back on. And that kind of told me: Hey, maybe there really is a fire in there. So I stop-cocked the engine. That airplane had never been landed dead stick, and I thought: Now I've got a problem. So I opened up the RAT, which is the ram air turbine, which supplied the hydraulics to get control to come down to land. And actually, as it turned out, I made one of the best landings I ever made in the F-100, and got on the ground.

Now [North American Aviation test pilot Bob] Hoover had had trouble at the company landing the F-100, using the ram air turbine. But Hoover was what we call a churner. He liked to feel the controls, and he was moving them all the time. As a test pilot, I never moved a control unless I wanted to move the airplane. There's nothing wrong with the other technique. A lot of pilots use it. Except that he was bleeding the ram air turbine hydraulics down. So he didn't have enough to flare, and he landed very hard in the two times he tried it, and damaged the airplane.

Well, I landed on my spot on the lakebed. With the rocket airplanes, I had eventually found where I could put it down. I'd roll out, turn up the ramp, coast up to the hangar door, and park it. Well, if I'd have been smart, I'd have left the F-100 out on the lakebed to be towed in. So I coasted up the ramp, and was in perfect position. Just was going to tap the brakes to stop it. The handbook says there are only three cycles on the brakes without engine hydraulics. I knew that. So I applied a little brake, but I didn't cycle back. And I thought: That's not a cycle yet. I applied a little more, and applied a little more.

If you go back and study the system, each one of those motions is a cycle. I used up all the hydraulics. So the last application, right in front of the hangar door — there were no brakes. So it went in the hangar door, and stuck it's nose out through the hangar wall. It's always been kind of a humorous incident. People thought I was injured, because I sat in the cockpit. What I was trying to do was to control my anger at being such a stupid jerk. Yeager always said, "The sonic wall was mine. The hangar wall was Crossfield's."

Q: We had a safety training class recently in that hangar, right near that corner of the hangar wall.

A: Everybody shows me that patch every time I go there. There's a little incidental thing that's funny there. I always make a joke. I hit right between the stanchion that held that 25 ton door balance weight and the controls for the 50,000 gallon water deluge system. That would have been a disaster to hit either one of those other stanchions.

Q: What led to your decision to leave the NACA?

A: The X-15. We had worked on the X-15 since about 1951. I was incidental in inventing the airplane, along with Walt [Williams] and Jake Drake. By the time we got a contract in 1955, I had made up my mind that unlike the X-2, that we needed an airplane to come in on time and to do what it was supposed to do. So I went to North American and worked in the design room on the X-15 for three years, took it into flight test in 1959, and did the company demonstration it would fly, and the systems would work, and that sort of thing.

Q: What were some of your contributions to the X-15 design?

A: Oh, golly. I worked in every area. Stability and control, power plants, propulsions. In fact, I even worked with the guy that designed that joint that broke in two. I knew where it was going to break. I didn't know why it was going to break. But I did an awful lot of work on the development of the cockpit and the pressure suit. There was a lot of firsts on the X-15. Worked a lot on the wind screens. Because we didn't know how we were going to get one that could stand the heat and we could see through. I worked for a long time on getting rid of an Air Force edict that we have an encapsulated escape system, which nobody believed in. But General [Thomas S.] Power had issued an edict that all future Air Force airplanes would have encapsulated escape systems, which would have sunk the X-15 to have to go to all of that. We had encapsulated escape in the D-558-II, and the D-558-I, and the X-2. And to my mind, and [Capt. Milburn] Apt pretty much proved it, this is the way to commit suicide to keep from getting killed. They never did have the development on them that they should have had, and they weren't any good anyway. If you could make a capsule that was good enough to live through the emergency, you might as well fly it and throw away the airplane.

"...the hangar wall was Crossfield's." Three views of the mishap on Crossfield's first F-100A flight on September 8, 1954. Workmen repaired both the hangar wall and the F-100. (The weld marks on the replacement sheet metal are still visible on the outside hangar wall, nearly 50 years later.) Crossfield went on to play a major role in solving the problem of inertial coupling in the F-100. (E54-1369, E54-1367 (inset), and E54-1366) (next page).

Q: So on June 8, 1960— Is that when you did the test of the XLR-99 engine in Ship 3 where it exploded?

A: Yes. We were running on the test stand, the last engine run before the first flight. Interesting enough, nobody had ever gotten ten minutes of un-incidental time on that engine, on the ground or anywhere, up until that time. We were going to go flat. The engine did not explode. It was our North American propulsion system that failed. And it was due to a long chain of events that we don't have time to do here. But it was a very explainable— The way that the emergency relief valve boot strapped itself up, my gauge pressure looked normal. So I didn't know anything was happening, even though the tanks were heading for a burst in pressure. And they did. It always kind of tickles me that I get in the cockpit, and everybody else gets in a block house. That's called building the confidence of the pilot. I understand that they never made a ground run with a pilot sitting in the cockpit after that. That amazed me. To be afraid of a manned airplane. I just can't understand that mind-set.

Q: So what did you do after the X-15 program?

A: I stayed with North American as Chief Pilot. I did the first flights on the T-39 for North American. At that time it was becoming abundantly obvious that aeronautics, as we had known it up to date, were heading for the doldrums. There was just nothing coming along behind it. All of the interest was in space, and that sort of thing. So I went over to Downey and worked on the Apollo program for Harrison Storms. Over there I owned all of the systems tests, reliability engineering, and quality assurance. It was a big organization. And while NASA got me fired off of that, I was convinced that I did my duty. We went to the Moon. And I had set up the disciplines that worked.

Q: And what are some of your thoughts on the value of the pilot in flight test? [There is] a real trend towards unmanned vehicles now.

A: If something is unmanned, I say, "The hell with it." This is a human endeavor we're living in. And unmanned systems — they're alright. They serve a purpose. We have automatic typewriters, and automatic transmissions, and that sort of thing. But I'm a pilot and an aviator. I think if we're going to do anything like go into space, or fly fast and that, it's pretty much an experience that a man wants to do. We're a human race, not made of machinery.

CROSSFIELD ADDRESSES ESCAPE SYMPOSIUM

"We know that attempted escape above 35,000 - 40,000 feet would probably prove fatal. We know that escape at speeds that are in excess of 500 knots would probably prove fatal," A. Scott Crossfield (Pilots) recently told 500 scientists, military personnel, aeromedical researchers, and industry engineers at an escape symposium sponsored by the Institute of Transportation and Traffic Engineering Extension, University of California at Los Angeles, in conjunction with the Aeromedical Engineering Association and the Institute of Aeronautical Sciences.

Crossfield also pointed out that the length of time which elapses between the development and production of new types of escape equipment must be drastically shortened.

"Expert talk," he said, "pride of authorship, and standardization are the bottlenecks in the flow of this equipment to pilots. We know that there are the means and, in fact, the hardware in existence to protect against loss of equipment and wind blast, but it is not available for us."

"We know," Crossfield continued, "that there are means with existing equipment to stabilize the free-fall spinning tendency, but it is not being provided us."

(For a complete coverage of the meeting, see AVIATION WEEK, October 24, 1955.)

From the pages of the X-Press.

BIRTH

CROSSFIELD - a son, Anthony Lawrence, born Thursday, April 16, to Mr. and Mrs. Scott Crossfield (Pilots), 6 pounds 15 ounces.

JACK FISCHEL
Telephonic interview by Dr. J. D. Hunley, September 20, 2000

Jack Fischel came to the High-Speed Flight Research Station in August of 1950, after nearly a decade at Langley. He participated in the inertial coupling research, following an incident involving the X-3 in October 1954. Of course, as Fischel recounts, inertial coupling was only one of the many unknowns explored during the 1950s. For instance, under certain conditions, the swept wings adopted for super-sonic flight also caused aerodynamic problems such as pitch up. If this phenomenon occurred during high speed flight, the aircraft could go out of control; if it happened during landing, the aircraft might stall and crash. The D-558-II (best known for high-speed research, including the first Mach 2 flight) played a key role in efforts to understand the mystery of pitch up.

Q: Jack, could you tell us a little bit about your family background and education and how you came to work for what is today called the NASA Dryden Flight Research Center.

A: Well, I grew up in a family of five, which includes my parents and a brother and sister. I was the youngest of the family (born July 1918), attended public school in New York City—this was the Borough of Bronx—and somewhere about the third or fourth grade my folks, who had been in the grocery business, purchased a store in Washington Heights, which is the northern part of Manhattan, at which time I transferred to a school there (P.S. 115), which provided education to the fourth grade. For the fifth and sixth grade I attended another school (P.S. 169). I felt I accomplished something in the way of improving my education— By the way, my family background is such that my parents were immigrants to this country. They had immigrated from Europe in the period of about 1905 to 1910, met in New York, and were married about 1912.

At any rate, going back to the schooling—I was a diligent scholar. And when I went to junior high school (which was seventh, eighth and ninth grades), starting at the seventh grade, I was placed in a rapid group, so that I accomplished the seventh grade in one-half year and the eighth grade in one-half year. And then the ninth grade, of course, was the first year of high school. I attended the seventh to ninth grades in a public school called P.S. 115 in Manhattan (the same school as in earlier fourth grade). Subsequently, I elected to go to George Washington High School. By the way, while I was in the seventh, eighth and ninth grades, there were a bunch of other advanced students in the classes with me, some of whom elected to go to Townsend Harris High School in New York City, which was a three-year type high school rather than four years. But since that was downtown, required spending money for car fare, etc, and my folks were not that affluent, I elected to go to George Washington High School in Washington Heights. I completed my education at George Washington High School in January 1935, taking the usual courses leading to a college education. And I earned good grades—without boasting, I think it was on the better side of good grades—and earned entrance to City College of New York, which was of generally high scholastic standing. At City College of New York I took some of the usual pre-engineering courses. Incidentally, they did have some engineering courses, but not in aeronautics or aerospace.

I attended City College full-time for a while—I think it was about one year plus—at which time my brother, who had been helping my folks in the family grocery store elected to go out and find a paying job because he also was a student and required funds. He was a chemical engineering student at New York University. So I worked in the family store and continued my education at CCNY at night. After about two years, I decided this was not getting me anywhere toward an aeronautical engineering degree. So, with the approval of the family—because this cost additional funds attending New York University—I attended New York University at night and continued my aero engineering course. I transferred to New York University in 1938, and by attending night course I took as many credits as I could. I was married in June of '41 and my wife and I decided that I should complete my education in one more year by going to day school rather than taking two years to continue at night.

Meanwhile, in 1939, I had taken an examination for the City of New York Police Department, mainly because jobs were scarce at that time. I had qualified by passing written and physical tests, and went on the appointment-waiting list. I continued attending night classes at NYU and working with my family in the grocery store. In the beginning of 1941, I received a call for an appointment as a patrolman with New York City and elected to accept that job, meantime continuing my education, attending evening classes. After the summer of 1941 I took a leave of absence from my patrolman position and signed up for the full year in day school at New York University. Meantime, my wife was working, helping me get through college. And in December 1941, of course, we were attacked by Japan. Classes after December 1941 were accelerated to the point that we graduated in April of 1942.

Now why did I elect aeronautical engineering? It had appeal to me. I can't say I had always wanted to be an aeronautical engineer. In my early days I thought, well, I would like to be a doctor. But, very frankly, I saw my folks could not afford that particular route so I elected to go with aeronautical engineering, which was my second best choice. Then about December '41 or maybe January of '42 recruiters from NACA visited the college. and tried to see if they could induce any of the qualified students to sign up. I signed up with NACA. I was intrigued with the work they did in aeronautical research. And in April of '42, soon after graduation, my wife and I moved down to Hampton, Virginia. Well, in Virginia it was really a new environment for me, as was getting acquainted with my colleagues at NACA. I was initially assigned to what was then called the Atmospheric Wind Tunnel, which had a seven-by-ten foot (testing area) tunnel that tested aircraft models. At that time, with the acceleration of effort caused by the war, we were operating around the clock. As one of the newest recruits, I took my turn at working night shift, day shift, any shift at all. My wife and I finally moved into a government housing unit called Langley View. We resided there for several years—this was from 1942 till 1946, at which time we purchased a house elsewhere in Hampton, Virginia.

Well, getting back to my work at the laboratory. I really enjoyed it no matter what shift I was on. One of the strange things for my wife and I, was we were without our own transportation for quite awhile. And since where we lived at Langley View was way back in the woods, it was about a mile to the main highway leading to town or

Langley Field. There was no transportation there, except early in the morning and late in the evening there was a bus that traveled back and forth, maybe a couple of times, from our housing project down to the main highway, which was the main road going between Hampton and the base—Langley Field. I did not have transportation to my work place, so we purchased a bicycle and a flashlight to mount on the bicycle. That's the way I wended my way to work in the dark hours. And it continued that way for about one year, until we saved to purchase a car.

Somewhere about mid-1946, we purchased our own house and moved into Hampton. But prior to that, it seemed to me that there was a new testing work section opening up in the west end of Langley Field. It was called the Seven-by-Ten-Foot Tunnel Section, having two new wind tunnels. They were higher speed, and essentially eclipsed the work that was done at the Atmospheric Wind Tunnel where I had been previously assigned. So I was reassigned and worked in that particular section and really enjoyed it—doing the work, designing models and equipment, testing military and research models, analyzing the data, writing the reports and reviewing reports of others, of course.

The engineering work involved the testing of models of current and planned aircraft, to ascertain their characteristics and to modify such models to improve their stability and controllability. Analysis of the data provided charts, graphs, and discussions which were included in classified and unclassified reports provided to "industry," as appropriate. In these research studies, we worked in "teams," initially supporting a group leader and later as the team leader. In the testing of research models — including semi-span wings or tail surfaces—we researched the effectiveness of various flaps, slats, aileron controls, wing fences, wing-tip extensions, etc—possibly applicable to a variety of aircraft. Also, we prepared a summary report on the characteristics/effectiveness of full-span flaps with various lateral control devices.

In the winter of '49, my wife became ill, could not be treated locally, and had to go to New York for treatment. She was in New York for about six months—had several surgeries—and I was home with the kids. (By that time we'd had two children - in '43 and '46.) My mother came south to Virginia to help take care of the kids. Also, my mother-in-law, who was in New York, looked after my wife in New York. During that period, I made several trips to New York to visit my wife in-and-out of her hospital stays. Well, when my wife came out of the hospital, about June of 1950, we were told by her doctors that we should get to a dry climate. The Hampton climate was not conducive to good health for my wife.

So we went looking to see what we could do to move to a dry climate. Shortly before that time, we heard quite a bit about the new NACA flight-test group starting out at Muroc. And I decided well, let's see what we can do about possibly going out there. Also there was a gentleman by the name of Robert Swanson, who was a former NACA employee, and had transferred to the Naval Research facility at Point Mugu some time before 1950. So I contacted this Robert Swanson to find out what was available on the west coast. He wrote back and offered me a job there. But I thought well, I'm not so sure I wanted to go there. I approached Hartley Soulé, who we used to call our "great white father"—he was Head of our Research Division at NACA, and he was also head of the Muroc group that was out at Edwards. I approached Hartley Soulé and asked, "Hartley, what do you know about Edwards (Muroc)? What can I do to get to Edwards? Tell me what it's all about." He explained to me what it was. He didn't paint any great pictures. He indicated it was kind of primitive, but if I really wanted to get out there, he'd see about that.

Sure enough, I guess he contacted Walt Williams to see if I could get transferred there. Well, I had previously known Williams at Langley. He worked in the Flight Division at Langley and our paths had crossed on several occasions, one of which was

A desert landscape near Lancaster. For Fischel and his wife, who had both been from New York City, life in the desert represented a major change. (E60-5342)

when I was testing an F6F airplane model in the wind tunnel and making an analysis and report on it. Meantime, Walt was the engineer in charge of testing an early version of the F6F airplane in flight. We'd seen the data that each other had from these tests. So I decided to accept this offer to go out to Edwards Air Force Base. (At that time it was just called Muroc.) And we moved west in August of 1950. It was quite a move, because we moved out west in the middle of the summer heat, and we drove cross country. Before leaving Virginia, we left our house in the care of a realtor, and purchased a car. We also decided to purchase one of these fandangled automobile air scoops that had a water reservoir, to see if we could keep cool during the trip. And we did. We trekked cross country in the car. When we arrived at Las Vegas, we decided it was so doggoned hot—we've got to do something better. So we decided we're going to awake in the middle of the night and travel in the cool hours, which we did, and we made our last-lap dash to Muroc—actually, to Mojave. We had been told that we would have "officer's quarters" at the Mojave Air Base. When we arrived at the Mojave Air Base, we reported in to the office that was in charge of the housing. And sure enough, they gave us what they called "officer's quarters." Well, I don't have to go into too much detail to tell you that was pretty awful. It was an apartment on a concrete platform with about three other apartments adjacent to it. They were built in groups of four. And the housing itself—the walls were made pretty thin, they were made of some prefabs of a sort. I wouldn't say it was wood. It may have been a combination of wood and cardboard. Anyway, it was not the most delightful place, not even marginal. At any rate, soon after that, I reported to work at Edwards and I met Walt Williams, De Beeler, a number of other people—Jake Drake. Jake, we used to call him—that was his nickname—but his name was Hubert M. Drake.

Q: Yes. He goes by Hubert now.

A: Right. Okay. He was known as Hubert then too, but we used to call him by his nickname, Jake. After some orientation and introductions, I was assigned initially as the engineer for one of the D-558-II [Skyrocket] airplanes. These were swept-wing airplanes which were sponsored by the Navy. There [were three different configurations] — one was an all-jet airplane, there was one that was a combination rocket and jet, and the third one was an all-rocket airplane. At any rate, I was assigned to [a D-558-II] with a combination rocket and jet. The D-558-II with the rocket-jet was taken aloft in the "belly" of a B-29. And then the research pilot, who was taken aloft inside the B-29, crawled into the D-558-II cockpit, closed the canopy—and after that when the B-29 arrived at the release point in time and location, the B-29 crew released the research craft. In the case of the rocket airplane, of course, it expended all its fuel in achieving whatever speed/altitude and maneuvers were necessary or called for, and then it became a glider, gradually descending. In the case of the rocket-jet airplane, the rocket part of the operation was much the same—after launch from the B-29, operate the airplane at as high a speed and altitude as you possibly could attain depending on the flight plan, performing various maneuvers on the way down. Of course, it was able to land under power because it had a jet engine. It was interesting.

The work was a little different, of course, than the wind tunnel research. The job was broader in scope in that we had to see that the airplane was properly instrumented for the research program at hand. Of course, there were technicians there who performed the instrumentation installation. Then we had the airplane and instrumentation checkout. There was also the flight crew who handled the preparation of the airplane for flight—made sure everything was working operationally. When we first arrived at Edwards, I believe they had about 50 employees at the NACA facility, which included technicians, mechanics in the shops, engineers, and computers. By "computers" I mean human-type who reduced the flight data. I liked the work. Oh, the base environment was kind of raw. I don't know if you've ever been down to South Base, but it was very primitive. We didn't complain because the research work was what was going on, and was important and enjoyable.

My family was not very comfortable living at the Mojave Air Base, and after many months of diligent search, we found a rental place in Lancaster to which we were able to move. About January or February of 1951 we moved into Lancaster, which made our surroundings much more habitable and more comfortable. Of course, that made it easier for us also. It was about 30-33 miles from our abode to the air base, which we

High-Speed Flight Station employees leaving work at the end of the day. As had been the case earlier at Langley, car pools became (and still are) a common practice in the remote terrain. This allowed the members to spilt the cost of gas, share the long drive, and enable their families to use the car for most of the week. (E54-1356)

had to drive initially every day. Subsequently, we formed a car pool and drove one day out of three or four or five, whatever it might be. And that, too, made it easier for us. That way, we could leave transportation most days for our family. Our work was very good, and about 1954, the NACA facilities expanded with the opening of a new building on "Main Base." More employees came. Of course, some left. One of the factors that we noticed during that period of time was that some of the engineers, as well as some technicians, didn't stay very long. The nature of the area (the environs) was such that it was just too raw for their families. Their families could not tolerate it for long. And I'll say this—I have to give my wife a medal and much commendation for putting up for all the period that we were there, because it was anything but excitable or appealing for anyone who was raised in the environments of New York City.

Well, about 1954 I believe it was, we were told that more employees were moving into the new NACA building. The construction had been going about a year or more. We moved to the new building, and it was much more comfortable—much more conducive to satisfactory operation. Also, we were closer to our work in the sense that the aircraft hangar was in the same building with all employees and the flight line was pretty close too.

Q: You had been in the separate Butler building before?

A: Oh, yes. I should have mentioned that. We had been in the separate Butler building at South Base. It was, you might say, the large, rounded-top building. Actually, our office portion was just on one side of the Butler building. And so we got along, of course. (We had to during those years.) During the period of 1950 to 1954, the scope of our work expanded. We were flight testing at that time the D-558's, the X-1's and the X-2's. Oh, yes, the X-5 was in our hangar too, at that time, and the X-4 too. Then after various phases of the D-558-II project, I recall writing a number of technical reports based on the results of the research flights. One of the things that we encountered was something called "pitch up." Pitch up was an uncontrollable response of the airplane when it attained a certain point with a high angle of attack (which varied with the Mach number). The pilot would not be able to control it properly, as the airplane would pitch up and the pilot would have to push forward on the control stick to get control again. We tried various devices on the D-558-II, such as wing "fences," leading edge slats, some changes in the flaps, different things in order to correct the situation. There was some degree of improvement resulting from some modifications, but not quite as much as we wished. We finally resolved that the location of the horizontal tail relative to the wing on the D-558-II made a great difference because of the "downwash" from the wing. Anyway, this goes into some technical areas of the work. Subsequently, we got into a new project on the X-3 airplane, which was a needle-nose airplane. I don't know if you've seen a photograph of it.

Q: Oh, sure.

A: Okay. It's a forerunner of the F-104 as it had a thin, very small wing of very small span, and the leading edge was swept back. The X-3 proved to be somewhat of a dud in the sense that I'd understood that it was originally designed to be higher-powered than it actually was. But it never did receive the engines that were supposed to be installed into it. It was a twin-engine airplane with rather low-powered engines which attained trans-sonic speeds (to about Mach 1.2)—not very high. At any rate, we evaluated that airplane with its different characteristics. We made some slight modifications to it—ran into another phenomena called roll-coupling.

Views of some of the fences and slat designs tested on the D-558-II #3 (NACA 145) to investigate the problem of pitch ups on swept wing aircraft. Some of the concepts proved effective; others actually made the pitch up worse. Although fences and /or slats eventually appeared on production aircraft, the ultimate solution to pitch up involved changing the position of the horizontal stabilizer. In the case of the D-558-II, it was mounted half way up the tail. On later aircraft, such as the F-100 and F-8, engineers repositioned the horizontal stabilizer low on the aft fuselage, below the wing and out of its downwash. (E51-0578, E51-582, E52-816, E52-817)

Q: Oh, yes.

A: Okay. At first we (my colleague, Dick Day, pilot Joe Walker) didn't know what the heck hit us—when the pilot performed a roll maneuver and suddenly seemed to lose control of the craft. We had by that time set up simulators and computers to simulate the action on the X-3 airplane and to evaluate the characteristics of the airplane. We found that the airplane was subject to roll coupling at very high angles of attack. And we noticed that some other airplanes were also subject to roll coupling. I believe the F-100 ran into that same phenomenon. And one of the things that was done, I recollect, was to increase the size of the [F-100] vertical tail (to improve directional stability). I believe that was the phenomena that some other airplanes experienced somewhere around the same time. We soon understood what was going on for some of those high performance aircraft.

I think I was involved with some other aircraft soon after the X-3. I believe it was an JF-107A. One of the things we were interested in investigating on the JF-107A was the X-15's side controller. There were things that we tried to foresee for the X-15 when we performed our research flights—anticipate the possibility that the pilot of the X-15 would not be able to properly control the airplane at all times with a center stick. So we thought well, we should investigate the use of a side stick in another airplane. So, I believe it was a JF-107A North American airplane, which was made available to us; and we were working on installing a side stick in the airplane. If I recall correctly, that was the first project that we had with pilot Bill Dana. He came in as a new pilot, and was assigned to oversee the installation of the side stick in the JF-107A and then try it out in flight. Well, I can't recall if that job was too successful. For some reason I can't remember how far we got into the actual research. (Perhaps Bill Dana can.) But anyway, the X-15 eventually did have a side stick.[1]

Oh, yes. There was one more thing too. One of the big questions that came up during those years was—this was when the jets were being developed by Boeing and Douglas. They were all developing commercial jets. One of the big questions that arose within the industry was how would you integrate them into the present system of air traffic control? In other words, we're still going to be flying these propeller airplanes for awhile until these jets take over. But how do you integrate this in that system? Where the jets are flying so much faster and also require more runway for takeoff and landing, how can you handle this sort of thing? So about 1958, I believe it was, the center obtained the loan of a KC-135 tanker from the Air Force. General LeMay relinquished that tanker to us for a three-month period. During that three-month period we evaluated the performance of a large jet aircraft in an operational status so that we could report to industry just what was going on. We received numerous requests from Eastern Airlines, American Airlines and other airlines with regard to what to expect from these aircraft.

So I prepared a program for testing the aircraft, submitted it and it was accepted. When the airplane arrived at the NASA facility, we spent about the first month or more instrumenting the airplane. We got our instrumentation people out there in a hurry and said this must be done rapidly, so that we could get the flight tests done within the three months and then return the airplane. Well, we got this aircraft instrumented. Then we started following the flight plan. Now some of the work that we did was on our own base (Edwards) for takeoff and landing and various other things. Other things that we wanted to do was go to a place like Los Angeles (LAX) or go to some other airports

A classic image of the X-3 in flight above Edwards AFB. Like the early F-100A, it also experienced inertial coupling. On October 27, 1954, at about the same time the NACA F-100 inertial coupling tests began, Joe Walker made a flight in the X-3. The test called for an abrupt left roll at Mach 0.92. As the aircraft rolled, it also pitched up 20 degrees and yawed to the side 16 degrees. The X-3 gyrated for five seconds before Walker got it back under control. He then decided to try the maneuver at Mach 1. When he made the abrupt left roll at supersonic speed, the nose yawed 21 degrees, which imposed a load of 2 Gs. At the same time, the aircraft pitched down (reaching a -6.7 G load), then pitched up violently to a +7 G measurement. Walker again brought the X-3 back under control and landed immediately. Post flight analysis of the data indicated the aircraft's fuselage had reached its maximum load limit. (E67-17348)

---

[1] Fischel recalled the aircraft used in the side stick tests as being an F-106. Richard P. Hallion's On The Frontier indicates it was an JF-107A.

Jack Fischel also worked on the North American JF-107A, shown here. This aircraft began as a modified version of the F-100, but evolved into a completely new design. The JF-107 featured a distinctive top-mounted engine inlet. Once the Air Force selected the F-105 for production, the service transferred the first and third F-107s to the NACA. The first aircraft proved mechanically unreliable, and made only four flights. The third JF-107A tested the X-15 side stick controller, designed to allow the pilot to fly the hypersonic aircraft during the high G-loads of re-entry. (E-4384)

and see how you can work-in the takeoff or landing along with the propeller-driven airplanes that were being used at the time, to see how the ground crews and the ground control could accept us and just how they'd operate. So this was part of our plan and we did just that. Within the two months remaining for flying, we had 17 flights or more that we performed on the airplane. These were long flights—three hours or more with the airplane. And we had the airplane in heavyweight condition, lightweight condition—all kinds—in order to see what the pilot and airplane could do when they got to takeoff, landing approach, aborted takeoff, wave-off, etc. Now we went to places like LAX and we did some landings and takeoffs, etc, there.

We also went to some other places including Oxnard Air Force Base, which is of course controlled by the military. And then we went to some other places also to do some takeoffs and landings. Oh, some of the things we measured were the takeoff and landing distances under various weight conditions. In addition to this sort of thing we asked our co-pilot to perform some tricks on the pilots, unbeknownst to the pilot, to see how the pilot could respond—such as cutting power abruptly during a takeoff and see how the airplane could be handled. Also doing something to the flaps so that the pilot wouldn't have full use of flaps during landing. Incidentally, Stan Butchart was the pilot and Jack McKay was the co-pilot for these tests. It was quite a successful program in the fact that we accomplished a good deal over quite a bit of time operationally. The other thing we did, too, was once the airplane got in the air, we asked the pilots to

A Boeing KC-135 military tanker used to test air traffic control procedures for the first generation of jet airliners that entered service in the late 1950s. The NACA borrowed the KC-135 to simulate the tanker's civilian equivalent, the Boeing 707 airliner, for a short but intensive series of flights which Fischel oversaw. (E-4123)

perform various maneuvers such that we could evaluate the performance and controllability of the airplane, such as its rolling performance, its side slip and maneuverability. This was quite a successful program, I felt. And when it came down to reporting the results, we had to whip them into shape because a NASA conference was planned (at Langley) in which various members of the aircraft industry as well as people in the airline business were invited to discuss the results. Well, I had some help, of course. I was not the lone engineer on the job. There were several others, and Butchart was the main pilot. So, between us, we wrote and reported to the conference two reports (papers) which reported on the characteristics of the airplane at high speed and also at low speed as well as takeoff and landing distances—that sort of thing. We presented them at this conference, and also they became NASA reports. I think the industry was relatively satisfied, and some of their uncertainties were laid to rest, although there were many questions at the time by industry representatives. Fortunately, the pilot could address most of those because they were the sort of questions that were aimed directly at the pilot. For example: how could the pilots handle this? What did they run into? And that type of thing. It was a good conference.

Q: Let me ask you—since our time is running out for this afternoon—about a couple of the people you worked with and for. I wonder, first of all, if you could characterize Walt Williams as the Head of the Center for the first nine years that you were there. What kind of a boss was he? How were your working relations with him?

A: Pretty good. Matter of fact, you know, he was unique in this sense. He had been through this before. He had known about flight testing before coming to Edwards. He had done this back at Langley. So he knew what had to be done and he depended a lot on the people under him, of course. They were people like Joe Vensel, who was in charge of Operations. Joe Vensel had been a test pilot years ago. But his ears, of course, had been "shot out" I guess by some of the work he had done. There was Gerry Truszyski, who had previously worked at Langley and who was in charge of Instrumentation. I recall being at various meetings at which we got together to discuss the problems and what to do about them, and so on. Beeler, of course, represented the Research Division in those early days. Then later on, that changed. But we got along pretty well.

Q: Well, good. Let me ask. When did you retire?

A: The end of June in '73.

Q: So you worked under Bikle actually longer than under Walt Williams.

A: Yes, I did.

Q: What did you think of Bikle as a leader and a manager?

A: Not quite the same as Walt Williams. Although he was a pilot, and so on, and he understood pilot things, I don't think he had the background of NACA-NASA. He had the Air Force background. I recall one time I had a little run-in with him, not because of him, himself, but because of something else. We had on base (Dryden) a Captain (medical) who was involved in pilot measurements and pilot response, during flight maneuvers and that type of thing. Anyway, he had made measurements on all the pilots as they flew their various maneuvers, and so on, and he was putting out reports. One of the things I did at that time was review reports, and I took exception to some of the things the way he was reporting in a report. One of the things we did, and I think we still do, is to have an editorial committee on every report. I don't know if that's still done.

Q: I think so.

A: Okay. I'd try to see about having certain people on each editorial committee who would be, let's say, more familiar with the specific type of work being done in that report, as well as some other diverse research engineers. That way I felt I could give some fair criticism. Well, one of the things I found in some of the reports that this Captain tried to publish was something I felt was not as clear as it could be. Maybe it was clear for him, being in that special field. He had a medical background. But I felt that to someone who was about to read it, it was not that clear. So I critiqued it that way. He wasn't happy with me. One time he brought it up to Bikle, and Bikle had me on the carpet about that and said "Do you have to review these reports?" I said "Well, it's been the custom over here at NACA for years and years before my time." I pointed-out the reasons and advantages of doing so. Apparently, in the Air Force the author would turn out his report without getting a review by a committee, so to speak.

So Bikle thought about it for awhile. I felt kind of lame facing him about this sort of thing, as though I had obstructed justice—obstructed the preparation of the report, you know. But Bikle said "Okay. Do what you want to." But to that extent I felt I was on the carpet there defending myself. But otherwise I had no run-ins with him or anything. He was pretty fair.

Q: Well, he was famous for what was called the Bikle barrel, and that was exactly the sort of thing you're describing.

A: Yes.

Q: What about Joe Weil—since you worked for him for awhile too?

A: Oh, not only did I work for Joe Weil—we graduated together.

Q: Is that right?

A: Yes. Since I was, you might say, older because I had gone to night school so much, I joined him my final year at New York University in day school. He had been a day school student all along. We both graduated together—we both went to NACA—though he reported for work one week ahead of me.

Q: Down at Langley.

A: Down at Langley, right. I transferred to Edwards well before he did. And we worked in the same division back at Langley too. Let's see. He was in a different section, but we were both in the same division. Anyway, he came to Edwards a couple of years I guess after I did—at least that.

Q: You mean the flight—

A: To Edwards. He went to Edwards a couple of years after I did. And so we got along very well. In fact, Joe would often turn to me about some questions about personnel—what did I think, and so on. And I'd give him my opinion for what it was. And we worked very well together. During the years after Weil arrived at Edwards, we worked together in the Research Division, sometimes competing with planned programs for research; and for several years, we each headed different research groups (sections) in the Research Division, prior to his appointment as Director of Research and my appointment as Assistant Director of Research.

Q: Was he still Director of Research when you retired?

A: That's right.

Q: Well, that's an interesting lifelong—well, not lifelong—but since student days relationship.

A: But looking back I'll say this. I've thoroughly enjoyed my working there, and I've always said my motto has been—I enjoyed my work and I got paid for it. What could be better.

Q: Dr. J.D. Hunley. We are continuing an interview that was done with Jack Fischel a few days ago. He had some afterthoughts that he wanted to add to his interview. So, Mr. Fischel, if you want to go ahead and start.

A: Okay. With regard to some of the work we did on the D-558-II airplane—we used the airplane as a test bed for various means of alleviating an instability at the higher angles of attack. We tried various things such as fences, slats, wing extensions going forward and other things in order to improve the stability. And we had minor results, you might say, minor improvements. Now all of these tests were really based initially on tests that had been done in wind tunnels on other models. So we tried to apply it in flight and see what effect it would have. But as I mentioned previously, we found that they did not have too much effect. Matter of fact, we found out that one of the things that was wrong with their plane at these high angles of attack where we had instability was the fact that the horizontal tail was located in the wrong place.

    I think I mentioned previously that the work on the KC-135 was a very short period. But it was a very intense period and we accomplished quite a bit during that period. One of the things that I did, too, was in order to get the feel for how the passengers on a airliner would react to the flying of a jet airplane as opposed to the preceding propeller airplanes, I climbed aboard. I went aboard one of the flights with our pilots for about a three to three hour plus flights, and we went to various airports to get my evaluation as a passenger on the plane. And, of course, my comments to the pilots were a result of that.

    Now speaking of pilots, there's one thing I wanted to make clear—that a good deal of the work that we did there was involved with the pilots too. We would have preflight meetings, post-flight meetings to get an idea what the pilots encountered, what they felt in the way of the behavior of the aircraft. This applies to all aircraft that we tested. I think the pilots added significantly to our remarks regarding the handling qualities of the various airplanes we tested.

Q: Well, you had wanted to say something about the technicians and the people in the shops as well.

A: Oh, yes. Yes. They were quite helpful, too, in the sense that they made inputs to us, particularly the instrumentation technicians, to improve characteristics that we didn't quite plan for. And as we went along, during the course of the flight programs, they made some valuable inputs there. In particular, I do recall some of the people there. We

Walter "Rebel" Harwell, the highly skilled chief of instrumentation, made many important contributions to a wide range of flight research projects. (E55-2137)

had a gentleman by the name of Rebel—that was his nickname—who was the head of the shop.

Q: Harwell was his last name.

A: That's it—Rebel Harwell. He was quite a character and a lovable guy. He produced from his shop things which we thought would never be possible. So I do want to acknowledge that. Plus, also, the instrumentation technicians and, of course, the flight crews. The flight crews I thought were superb—everyone cooperative, working all kinds of hours—particularly the crew in preparation for a flight in the early days when we had the B-29 as the mother ship for the D-558-II and later on when we had the B-52 as the mother ship for the X-15. I have to say that these crews were terrific. They worked overtime as necessary, came in early, as necessary, in order to get off an early flight. So it was a tremendous esprit de corps there among our crew. I hope it still exists today, though I don't know. I just want to emphasize that. I thought it was an ideal place to work. Despite the fact that many people came and left because of the fact maybe their families were unhappy being in the desert, I'd say those who stayed were grateful they did and benefitted in the long run by the experiences they had. I think that's about it.

From the pages of the X-Press.

```
SCOOP OF THE DECADE

    THE PERSONNEL OFFICE IS HAPPY (AND RE-
LIEVED) TO ANNOUNCE THAT "REBEL" HARWELL AFTER
11 YEARS AND 1 MONTH AND TRUMAN PUGH, AFTER
6 YEARS, 3 MONTHS, AND 4 DAYS, HAVE AT LAST
BECOME CAREER EMPLOYEES.  INCIDENTALLY, REBEL,
WE COUDNN'T HELP IT IF YOUR SON COULD DO IN
3 MONTHS WHAT IT TOOK YOU 11 YEARS TO DO!
CONGRATULATIONS!!!!!
```

STANLEY P. BUTCHART
Interview by Curt Asher, September 15, 1997

As the 1950s drew to a close, the hard won advances in aviation technology found their way into production aircraft. Speeds which only a few years before had been world records now became routine in operational military aircraft. At the same time, new jet powered airlines had speeds and altitudes nearly double those of propeller airliners. Many of the unknowns of the late 1940s and early 1950s had become understood. NACA research pilot Stanley P. Butchart had been a participant in much of this activity. He served in the Navy as a torpedo plane pilot, then went to the University of Washington (the same school attended by research pilots Scott Crossfield and Milt Thompson) for his B.S. degrees in aeronautical and mechanical engineering. Butchart then worked as a Boeing engineer on the B-47, an airplane he would later fly as a research pilot, before joining the NACA in 1951. He flew the D-558-I and X-4, undertook pitch up studies in the X-5, served as the B-29 drop pilot for both the X-1 and D-558-II, and made flights in a KC-135 tanker (the Air Force version of the Boeing 707 airliner) to develop air traffic control procedures for jet airliners.

Q: I'd like to start by asking you a little about your personal history. When and where were you born?

A: Well, I was born in New Orleans, Louisiana on March 11, 1922.

Q: Did you grow up there?

A: No, the folks left there when I was about just past a year. They moved to Chicago, and then eventually out to Spokane where I spent the next 20 years.

Q: Do you recall what initially inspired your interest in aviation?

A: Well, I don't know. I think kids at that age were kind of thrilled with aviation. You know just going out to the airport and watching people fly and airplanes fly and what not. But I think my real interest came after I graduated from high school. I found out that they were giving that civilian pilot training (CPT) to the young folks at that time through the colleges. So I went to the Spokane Junior College and signed up for that.

Q: Did you pursue any aviation-related interests in your youth outside of the things you just mentioned?

A: Do you mean like model airplane building and that sort of thing?

Q: Yes.

A: Yes, very much so.

Q: Could you describe your Navy career for me? When and where did you enlist?

A: Well, I went to junior college to get that CPT training. Also I think about the same time I had a real desire to go in the Navy, which required two years of college. So I was going to get my two years at the junior college and enlist in the Navy. But the war came along and kind of speeded things up. It was kind of interesting. A buddy of mine who was also very much interested in aviation wanted to follow the same path. We were going out to college one morning on the bus and I read in the paper that the Navy had dropped their two-year college requirement. So we got off the bus, went back home and got a few things, and hitchhiked over to Seattle to enlist in the Navy. I grew up in Spokane, so we went over there to enlist. That was about May, I think. I had trouble with my birth certificate because they didn't like the looks of the piece of paper I had from New Orleans. It didn't look like a birth certificate. So they sent me home and had me write back to New Orleans and get a proper birth certificate, [and] they sent the same thing back. So finally I enlisted in July I think — July 8th. But I kind of sat around the rest of the summer waiting for this friend of mine to get his CPT training. He hadn't had the training. I had gone through primary and secondary CPT when I was going to the junior college.

Q: I see. What was your friend's name?

A: Les Jones.

Q: Les Jones.

A: Yes. Then they sent him over to Montana to get his primary CPT training. Then we both left October 1, 1942 to pre-flight school up at St. Mary's College there in California, it's right there near Oakland.

Q: So that was your military flight training?

A: Yes, it was. And it was kind of fortunate the way we did it. I kind of knew what was going to happen. When they dropped the two-year college requirement, there were thousands of people running to enlist. I kind of got in on the front wave of the thing. So I went through the Navy flight training in about nine months, with ten weeks of pre-flight school, and three months of basic, and three months of advanced.

Q: What was the flight training like? What was the daily routine?

A: Well, then the Navy had what they called the Yellow Perils, the N3Ns or the N2S trainer biplanes that we flew. The primary part of it was first just checking out in the airplane and then a lot of acrobatics, a lot of training for precision flying, some formation flying, some night flying. That lasted just about three months, I think, at primary. Then we went down to Corpus Christi, Texas for advanced training.

Q: So where were you stationed after you completed training?

A: Well, in the Navy, when you get your wings, you're sent off to an operational squadron. In my case I was sent to Opa-Locka, Florida for what they call operational training. Then you're training in a specific mission that you're going to be in — either fighters, dive bombers or torpedo bombers. I had been assigned torpedo bombers when I was back at Corpus. It wasn't my first choice, but you get to love it. So we went to Opa-Locka for our operational training and that lasted about six, seven weeks. And then from there, Navy pilots were sent mostly to the Great Lakes area— the Glenview Naval Air Station. The Navy actually had two carriers on the Great Lakes. They were converted coalers [with] side wheels. All they had was a flat deck on top, no superstructure above the [deck], and there was no facilities to live on them or stay on them. You just went out during the day and made your eight landings. You'd land, they'd roll you back, you'd take off and come around the pattern to do it again. Once you made your eight carrier landings you were qualified, then traditionally everybody got 30 days leave after that.

Q: So after your leave were you stationed on a carrier then or -

A: Well, yes. My orders when I left Glenview were to report to Norfolk in September of '43. After a few days there I was assigned to a torpedo squadron that was just being commissioned. It was actually a composite squadron. When it first started it had nine torpedo planes and nine dive bombers.

Q: What was the squadron number?

A: VT-51. We trained at Chincoteague, Virginia to start with.

Q: When you went overseas, how many combat missions did you fly?

A: Well, the Navy didn't really list them as combat missions like the Air Force did. I had some 30 different strikes against enemy installations, mostly island installations.

Q: In the South Pacific?

A: Yes, in the South Pacific. I had about 80 or 90 different anti-sub patrols — which we flew almost daily off the carrier.

Q: What decorations did you earn?

A: I got a DFC [Distinguished Flying Cross] for an operation on the 25th of October '44 when they hit the Japanese fleet that had come down from the Sea of Japan. In fact I dropped two torpedoes in one day, the first one on the carrier Zuikaku and later in the afternoon on the carrier Hosho. I got hit in the afternoon. Just after I dropped a torpedo I got hit in my right wing and knocked about four or five feet off the end of the wing. But I was able to get the thing back to the carrier.

Q: Could you tell me about some other combat incidents that you were involved in during the war?

A: Well, yes, there's a lot of interesting ones. But I think actually torpedo bombers — the guys that were trained in torpedo bombing — probably less than ten percent of them ever dropped a torpedo in anger. They all had dropped them in practice. Torpedoes were mostly saved for battleships, carriers and cruisers. The Japanese held their fleet back to home port for so many years that there was not much opportunity. But I had the opportunity of dropping four different torpedoes, one when we went to Okinawa on October 10th of '44. Reports were that there was a part of the Japanese fleet was there. When we got there, there was nothing but cargo ships. And so I dropped a torpedo on an old cargo ship and then the two I dropped on October 25th. Then later that month, we were up at the northern end of the Philippines into the Manila area. We went in there expecting to find a lot of shipping. And I had to wind up dropping the torpedo on a dry-dock, which isn't much of a target.

Q: No.

A: October was probably the most hectic month I've ever had in flying off the carrier. I flew 82 and a half hours in one month, which is a lot of flying, even off of land. We were busy the whole month supporting MacArthur's landing on Leyte on the 20th of October, and then the big battle with the Japanese fleet on the 25th, and then back down to Leyte supporting the landing some more.

Q: Can you think of anything else about your military career you might want to mention?

A: Oh I don't know. It was interesting. After the war was over, I was admitted to the University of Washington. I saw an article in the paper where they were forming Naval Reserve squadrons. So I hustled out to Sand Point and signed up to spend the next four or five years flying with the Naval Reserve group in Seattle.

Q: So you said you went to the University of Washington.

A: Yes, after the war.

Q: What degrees did you earn there?

A: Interestingly enough, I wound up at school with Scott Crossfield. He had been in the squadron with me. Our second tour — after we came back from overseas the first time, we got home on the 23rd of December to San Diego. They hustled us through all the checkpoints to get us out of there so we could get home for Christmas, which I didn't quite make. But then the squadron re-formed the second time in Seattle. Scott showed up there as a fighter pilot, having come from an instructor pilot down at Corpus. So we spent the next six, seven, eight months together in the squadron. Then when I started at the University of Washington he was in my class, and spent the next four years with me. We got our degrees in aeronautical engineering in June of '49. And then I went back to school that fall and got a degree in mechanical engineering.

Q: A Master's Degree?

A: No, just another B.S. in Mechanical Engineering. Scott went on to get his Master's.

Q: Let me just ask you another personal question. Are you married? And was meeting your wife related in any way to your career?

A: Yes, it sure was.

Q: What's her name?

A: Miriam. I met her on October 15th of 1943 right after the squadron was stationed at Chincoteague. The closest town to Chincoteague where we could go in for liberty was Salisbury, Maryland. And I met her in Salisbury. She worked for a jeweler in Salisbury.

We dated all that fall, and then the following spring, just before I went overseas, I asked her to marry me and gave her a ring. Then we were married after I got back from overseas. In fact, four of us were all married within a week or two when we got back. We were married on January 5th of '45, George and Barbara Bush were married on the 6th, Lou and Connie Grab was on the 20th, Jack and Eve Raquepaw was on the 13th. So the whole bunch of us got married, and Jack Guy later that spring.

Q: Were you a friend of George Bush?

A: Yes. He was in the squadron with us.

Q: What kind of a person was he?

A: Well, I'm asked that a lot. My recollection is that he was a very quiet fellow, very quiet. I was surprised years later to read some history about him and find out that he had a pretty large family of brothers and sisters. He really never talked much about his family, although I had met his mother when we were up in Charlestown, Rhode Island during January of '44. They lived in Greenwich, Connecticut. She came over and spent the entire day with us while we were training. He was a very quiet, very unassuming fellow at that time.

Q: You didn't have any indication that he would go into politics?

A: No, heavens no.

Q: Do you have any children?

A: I have four. The oldest one is Debbie. She was born in Seattle before we came down here in '49. Then a boy, Dean was born right after we moved to Lancaster in '51. Dierdre was born in '55 and Dale in '56.

Q: Okay. Have you maintained a cordial relationship with George Bush over the years?

A: Yes, indeed. I have a letter from him here. A couple of months ago where he was thanking Jack Guy and I for coming to his aid about the time he made that parachute jump back in April. There was an article written in the "Washington Times" by some lady that had never gone back and bothered to check the facts of a previous report that had been in the papers, in I think it was in '88 or '89 when he was running for President, about a comment about him. It was made by one of the guys in the squadron, a crewman who wasn't a regular assigned crewman to the airplane. But he flew with him that day. His comment was that George never should have jumped out — that he should have stayed with the airplane and he could have saved the other two fellows. But that isn't so. He wasn't close enough to see or know anything about it. George told us he stayed in there as long as he could, but it was just too hot — he had to climb out. Yes, and then we got an invitation just last week to the dedication of the Presidential Library which is taking place in Texas in College Station in November.

Q: That's great. After graduating from college, did you immediately go to work for the NACA?

A: No. I really had thought I was going to go to work for Boeing. I wanted to get into Boeing's flight test. But it's kind of a closed club and pretty hard to get your foot in the door. So I was assigned as a junior design engineer to the B-47 body group.

Q: At Boeing?

A: At Boeing. And after about six, seven months of that, I knew I didn't want to spend the rest of my life over a drawing board. I had kept in touch with Crossfield. He came down to NACA in the summer of '50. He told me then, "Hey, there's a lot of engineering jobs down there." I said, "No, I won't go down to the desert and be an engineer." I said, "But if a flying job opens, give me a call." Well, the following January I got a call from him one night and he said, "Hey, we've got an opening." So I re-filed my form 57, and by March I was invited down for an interview and had a job.

Butchart began flights in the D-558-I on October 19, 1951. He made twelve flights in all, the last one on February 20, 1953. The flights shed light on lateral stability and dynamic longitudinal stability. (E51-713)

Q: So that was January 1951?

A: Well, I came to work here on May 10th of '51.

Q: Was it an extremely competitive process getting a job as a NACA research pilot?

A: No, I don't think it was competitive. I don't know how many applications they had before them to look at. But like so many other things, if you know somebody on the inside it helps.

Q: So was there testing?

A: No, no. I just got a phone call one day at work asking if I could come down for an interview. I grabbed a TBM out of the reserve squadron and flew down to L.A. and stopped. [Joe] Vensel picked me up down there. I spent the day out at NACA, and when I left I had a job.

Q: So you were working for the NACA before it expanded to the present location in 1954. Could you describe what it was like working on the South Base in the early

Remains of Butchart's F-84 canopy. A faulty latch caused it to separate while Butchart took off on a familiarization flight in the aircraft. This was only the third time he had flown an F-84. (E51-0496)

'50's? What were the working conditions like?

A: Well, it was far from what we have now. In fact, the old hangar and the buildings are still sitting down there. But the pilots were — four of us — I made the fourth one when I showed up. We were all in a very small office. I think there were two operations engineers in the same office with us. But the nice thing about it — it was almost like family. The majority of the people lived in Lancaster and you knew each other. You played softball together, you bowled together, just the whole thing. I think there were only 185 people when I started there. It was a real nice congenial outfit to work with.

Q: So what was your day to day routine like there? Do you remember?

A: Well, it surely wasn't structured at all. Other than the days that you were assigned flights, you could go out and do proficiency flying any time and as much as you wanted to. And that was really all the activities there were in those days.

Q: And where did you live? Did you live in Lancaster?

A: I've lived in this house 46 years.

Q: Oh okay. In 1954 after the Dryden facility construction was complete, how did your day to day work routine change?

A: Not a whole lot. I think we were getting busier in those days with more airplanes coming in. Early on we had just two or three of the X airplanes. We had the X-4, the X-5, and the [D-558-I] Skystreak and the [D-558-II] Skyrocket. That was about the extent of the research airplanes that we had when we were down at South Base. We had a couple of proficiency airplanes. We had an old F-84 — one of the earlier airplanes — number seven I think. I lost a canopy on the third day I flew it.

Q: Is that right? How did that happen?

A: Well, it didn't lock properly. The canopy was not a clam shell. It was the kind that slid forward, and it had electric switch. When I held the switch, it looked like it was closed. As I started my takeoff roll, it started to open a little bit. I could feel the air blowing in on my face. I reached up and hit the switch again and it seemed to close.

After I got airborne it backed off a little bit again and more air was coming through and hitting me in the face. So I was leaning down to try to see what was wrong with the latches. And fortunately I was leaning down, I think, because they had a history of those canopies swiping like that as they came off. I had my head down looking to see what was wrong with the latching mechanism, and boom, it was gone.

> **NEW FACES**
>
> Three new employees have joined HSFS personnel within the last two weeks: Neil A. Armstrong, Aeronautical Research Scientist, assigned to Flight Operations, transfer from Cleveland; Barbara A. Hoag, Clerk-Typist (Receptionist), of Edwards; and Rodolfo J. Alvarado, ANGUS, assigned to Loads, from Laredo, Texas.

From the pages of the X-Press.

Q: Would you consider yourself one of the second wave of research pilots that was hired then?

A: No, I'd say the first wave. Because early on when they first came out to Langley and they were still part of Langley, they would bring a pilot out from Langley and they would be here for a year. Bob Champine spent a year, and I don't know who else. Champine was just going back to Langley when Scott came down in '50. Herbert Hoover, who was kind of a senior pilot at Langley, did some of the early flying on the X-1. In fact, he was the first civilian to fly supersonic after Yeager. But he would not stay out here. He'd come out on a C-45, stay a few days, make a flight and go back. And the next month he'd come out and do it again. So when they were starting to expand, there was Crossfield, and then they hired Walt Jones that fall. The next spring Joe Walker and I came on and made the four. That was about the minimum they needed to operate with. Because we inherited the B-29 drop airplane from Douglas that summer, and it took at least three of us, two in the B-29 and one in the research airplane, to carry on those operations.

Q: Did you work with Neil Armstrong?

A: Yes, in fact, I met Neil in a chow line back at Langley. I was back there for some meeting in the spring of '55. There were pilots down from Cleveland. They had four or five pilots. Ed Gough, as I remember, said, "Hey, I want you to meet this young fellow." He introduced me to Neil, and later on in the day he got me aside and he says, "Hey, you got any openings out there at Edwards?" I said, "I don't know. I'll have to ask Joe." He told me, "We hired Neil knowing we didn't really have an opening for him. But his scholastic record was so high we didn't want to pass him up." So after I got home, I talked to Joe Vensel and Walker and told them that this guy was out at Cleveland and was interested in coming out. Some paperwork transpired, and Neil showed up out at our place in May, I think, of '55. He flew with me as co-pilot on the B-29 on some flights, and co-pilot on the B-47, and I dropped him a few times too in some of the research airplanes.

Q: What was he like? What can you tell me about his personality?

A: Well, Neil was a very quiet fellow. He kept to himself an awful lot. A lot of people really never did get to know him. He was a bachelor when he first came to work out there. I've forgotten just where he was living. But he would come over to the house here and spend time with us. My daughter remembers him helping her with her math when she was going down here to Parkview School. He was kind of interesting too. Because when he was getting ready to get married or think about it, he asked me about how Miriam had felt about moving out to the west, coming from the east coast, because he was going to go back east and marry Jan and bring her out here. We talked it over and you know if she wants to make the move, why, she will.

Q: Who were some of the other people you worked with that you could tell some stories about? Maybe you could give me some sense of their personalities. For example, Scott Crossfield. I know you worked with him.

A: Lots of people didn't get along with Scott, He kind of rubbed them the wrong way. He had a different personality. He wasn't arrogant, but he was very positive. He said what he thought. And sometimes he was on the outside of the envelope with his thinking which is good. But he didn't get along with a some of the other pilots.

Q: I see.

A: Scott and I always had a real nice close relationship. He still comes by here maybe once a year and stops and visits, and we have dinner together. There was kind of a conflict between Joe Walker and Scott. I think part of the problem — my opinion again — was that Joe Vensel never was a division boss at that time. He did not appoint a chief pilot per se. He didn't say, you know, on paper or say that you're going to be the chief pilot. Scott rather assumed he was because he had been at Edwards before Joe Walker showed up. Joe Walker came out nine months after Scott. But he'd been with NASA at Lewis in Cleveland for four or five years. So he felt senior, and there was kind of a competition between the two of them.

Q: What about some of the other people that you came across?

A: Well, the four of us were together for just a year or two. And then again because of Scott, Walt Jones left. He went over to work for Northrop and he later got killed in an F-89. But he just could not get along with Scott that well. So he left, and we hired Jack McKay. Jack McKay had been an engineer. He did what Scott wanted me to do — be an engineer. Then a year later, after he had the opening, he hired him. So then there was four of us. We were together about three or four years and did nearly all of the flying on the rocket airplanes, which was our main operation at that time. Because we had pretty much finished up with the [D-558] Phase I and the X-4. I still had a program on the X-5 that ran for another year. Then after that, I guess Neil was the next one that came on board. He then made our fifth pilot. Then Bill Dana joined us. Milt Thompson may have been in between there, I can't remember. Milt was a University of Washington graduate also. He was a year or two behind Scott and I.

Q: Did you know Chuck Yeager pretty well?

A: Oh, commenting on Chuck. I don't know — we were never very close at all. I just didn't care for his attitude.

Q: Okay. Would you say that it takes a certain kind of personality to do the kind of work you do? How would you describe that personality? And how did that personality manifest itself in some of the people you worked with?

A: Well, I think any job in test flying — whether it be NASA, or the Air Force, or the company pilots — I think one of the main things is dedication. You've got to believe in what you're doing, and be dedicated to it, and love to fly if you're going to do that sort of work.

Q: So can you recall how that dedication manifested itself in some of the other people you worked with? Can you give me an example?

A: Well, I think just in the work that we did, and knowing what the risk involved. We

The High-Speed Flight Station softball team on the front steps of the main building. In the front row, left to right: Ed Holleman, Tom Cooney, Gene Kenner, George Miller, Dick Music, Bob Lyda; back row: Terry Larson, Jim Huffman, Chuck Lewis, Al Grieshaber, Tom Finch, Jack Russell, Al Brown. NACA personnel organized many sports teams, including basketball and bowling. (E56-2297)

never really thought of it as much of a risk. But you know that those early airplanes like the X-1's, the Skyrocket, Skystreak — none of those had ejection seats. They had a piece of paper showing us the speed and altitude envelope where you would be safe to get out. You got out of those things [the D-558 aircraft] by pulling one handle which dropped the nose of the machine off — then another handle that would release your little back rest and you kind of crawled out the back. That's not much of a way to get out of an airplane when you're in trouble. The envelope was rather restricted too as far as speed and altitude. When you stop to think of it, [at] the higher speeds, and you drop the nose off, you're going to get a very big negative G as you come out of there. So that restricts you as to how fast you can be going and still use that escape method. We would look at that and kind of throw it in the back of the desk and go on about our work.

Q: So what did you do then to ease the stress and tension of where you worked? For example, maybe you could just describe what you did for entertainment in the early years out there.

A: Well, I bowled with the NASA bowling team for five or six years. Bill, Walt and I were on it, one of the painters was on it, a couple of mechanics were on it, an inspector was on it. It was just made up of the family. We would play softball and had a couple of softball teams. Somehow if you'd drive clear back to Edwards in the evening you could play softball. Small groups would get together for picnics on their own besides the NASA picnic. It was that sort of thing. It was more of a family life for the whole group.

Q: People must have dropped by quite a bit and visited and that kind of thing.

A: Somewhat. I can't even remember what the activities were. But I remember my wife and Kleinknecht, who was in our operation here, would swap baby sitting when the Kleinknechts wanted to go down below, which was a big event in those days. They would sit for us when we would be out.

Q: So heavy drinking and that kind of thing, was that part of the —

A: No, no. It was more of just a big family life. There wasn't any big parties or anything like that. Later on, after the X-15 program [started], they would usually have some celebrations for the guy who made the first flight. Like I remember when Neil did and when Pete did and McKay and different ones like that. But that was about the extent of it.

Q: So, Dryden is said to have unique decentralized and unstructured management methods. Do you think it deserves its reputation? And, if so, can you give me some examples of ways in which management at Dryden was unique?

A: Well, I guess I never thought of it as being like that at the time, but it was. Again, I think it stemmed from the history of the people that came out here in the beginning. Walt Williams came out with just that small group. So many of them had known each other for a long time back at Langley. He brought Vensel out from Cleveland. But Vensel had been a test pilot at Langley back in '39, '40, through the war period. So they knew each other so well I think they just let them do their thing.

From the pages of the X-Press.

Q: I see. Do you think that it takes a certain kind of personality to find satisfaction working in a management capacity out there?

A: Well, it depends on how it works from the top down. Under Paul Bikle I found it very enjoyable to work there and Walt Williams before that. The thing I found with Paul — and I think this is a mark of a good manager too — if you went to him to ask him for a decision, or you had a question on something and you wanted him to make a decision, you'd better have all the answers when you went in there. If you did, and he could ask you questions and he was satisfied, you got the decision right then. But if you didn't have all the answers, you'd go back and do some more homework. But once you caught on to how he operated like that, it was real easy. And he'd pretty much let you do your thing.

Q: Was there ever any tension between the Air Force and the NASA flight test programs?

A: Maybe just a little bit. It's always irked me too that — I hate air shows and I hate setting records for records sake alone. You know if you get it in the step by step process of advancing an airplane — fine. But too many times out there, the streets are named for the guys that were doing this — you know Mel Apt and the rest of them. The Air Force was strictly trying to set a speed record., and they lost the X-2 for that very reason. Joe Weil I remember was head of our research group at that time. And he and another fellow that worked with him sat with the Air Force and told them on that last X-2 flight, "Don't do it. We're running out of directional control." But the Air Force knew that was going to be their last flight. They were going to have to turn the airplane over to the NACA. And they were going to go all out, and they did.

Q: Could you trace out your career at the Flight Research Center for me? I mean just kind of go through it chronologically. After being brought on board, what project were

Like Crossfield, Butchart also made research flights in the Bell X-5, but Joe Walker was the primary project pilot in the aircraft. Here, the X-5 is shown in front of an NACA hangar. (E53-1025)

you first assigned to, and how long did you work on that one?

A: Well, quite often you had two or three different things you were working on at the same time. When I came there I had always been a single engine pilot. I remember Crossfield took me out after I had been there a few weeks to check me out on the C-45. And that was kind of like the blind leading the blind, because he had never been much of a multi-engine guy either. So I checked out in the P-51, which was my first fighter plane to fly, and then the C-45 which we had as a transport. Then that F-84 was the first jet that I flew. Then from there on you just kind of had to wait your turn. Joe Walker was flying the [D-558] Phase I when I got there — he and Walt Jones. When they got a few flights in it and were moving on to something else, then I inherited the Phase I Skystreak. I had it for about a year or two with different programs on it. But in those days, sometimes the airplane would be down five or six months while they re-instrumented or reconfigured it for some other future flights they were going to do. I remember the Phase I — I flew it a couple of times in the fall of '51 and I didn't fly it again until the following summer. So they were few and far between.

But NACA was getting the [D-558-II] Skyrocket assigned to them. And that was the reason they needed another pilot, because the B-29 was going to come with it. That's kind of interesting when you think now how many months and months that pilots go to ground school to get checked out in a new airplane. We inherited the B-29 one afternoon when George Jensen, who was the Douglas pilot that had been flying it, called up Joe Walker and I and said, "Hey come on down and I'll give you a flight." They were right next door to us, actually. We went out flew the thing for about an hour or so, and made a couple of landings in the lakebed. And it was our airplane, and we were multi-engine airplane drivers. Joe was in the left seat when the first couple of drops were made and I was the co-pilot. Then within a few months he kind of turned the B-29's over to me. And for the next five years the biggest workload I had was flying the 29's. Then from there I got some flights in the X-4, and then after I had the X-5 program.

Q: You flew that plane [the X-5] thirteen times between 1952 and 1955.

A: Yes.

Q: What was it like to fly that?

A: Well, they were all interesting. They all had their little idiosyncrasies that you had to be aware of. If somebody else had flown first, why you could get this stuff from him. Otherwise you found out by yourself. But they all had some funny things. The speed brakes on the X-5 were up front [on the nose]. When you opened the speed brakes, you got quite a nose down pitch. Well, now it would be very unacceptable. But in a research airplane you put up with it because it's all you've got.

Q: But it had some design flaws.

A: Yes, it did.

Q: It had stall speed instability?

A: It had a bad spin characteristic too. Walker got into a spin accidentally. I don't remember what he was doing though — early in the program. And he fell about, I don't know, 25,000 feet or something before he got out of the [spin]. Then, this is another example of Crossfield. He went up. He was flying it and knowing that it had this bad spin, he poked into the same area and got into a spin — which was uncalled for. You just had to know that and stay away from it. That's what killed [Maj. Ray] Popson in the other X-5 that the Air Force was using.

Q: What kind of research were you doing with the X-5?

A: We were still doing some of the stability control with it. But I think one of the main things that I got into — it had this nasty pitch up that nearly all our swept-wing airplanes in those days had. A lot of the work that we did was investigating the pitch up, and learning how to live with it, and try to use it even in some of the later airplanes. But the wing had a kind of glove. When it swept, this glove covered part of the inside of the wing where the hinge was. They wondered if that was causing a lot of the airflow that was contributing to the pitch up problem. So they modified it and fixed the wings at 45 degrees, and then filled in with balsa wood to make a smooth transition over the wing. And that's why I flew quite a number of times just with the wings fixed at 45 [degrees] going through the same investigation for pitch up areas.

Q: What other X planes were you involved with?

A: Well, the only other ones were the X-4, and then the Skystreak and the Skyrocket. I flew the Skystreak about a total of twelve times.

Q: Do you remember what the focus of that research was?

A: Yes. Part of it was doing a lot of high speed rolls. I don't remember exactly what we were looking for then. Tom Sisk was the engineer on some of the later flights. He had a program where he was trying to look at aileron reversal. Aileron reversal on an airplane can be predicted by certain parameters that you look at I guess. So you have to get out to a pretty high speed to investigate the aileron reversal. It was difficult to do it, because it took most of the gas. It only had 202 gallons in the thing. Nowadays they call all that pounds. But that one had gallons. It took you quite a bit of the tankage just to get the altitude. And you'd get just as high as you could, and then milk it over to try to get speed by dropping your nose, without getting down so far that you were getting into denser air early on. So it was kind of a game to play. Once you'd get out to speed, then the only maneuver you had to do was just to crank the wheel over just as hard as you could. And from the measurements of the data they could tell whether there was any aileron reversal apparent.

Q: I see.

A: Aileron reversal was more apparent in some of the earlier planes like the B-47. It had a bad case of aileron reversal. It killed [Capt.] Joe Wolfe [and his crew] out there in '51. But that was another interesting program. I had that one for quite a few years. Joe Walker and I went to ground school on the B-47 in Wichita, Kansas in the spring of '52. It was kind of ironic, because a year earlier I was working at Boeing on the drawing board with the B-47, and a year later I'm flying the thing. We were there about two or three months. They put us through a T-33 instruments school first, and then the B-47. We had our choice of the 47 we were going to get. We could either pick one of the early models that they had there at Wichita, or wait for a B model. After talking it over, we decided to stick with the A model. In fact we had the number one A model — 1900. Because they had ejection seats in them. Later on the B-47's did not have ejection seats in them. We thought for our test work that was better. So it was flown back to Langley and was there about nine months I guess, before Joe and I brought it out here in March of '53. Then we flew it for another four or five years.

Q: Can you describe what happened on August 8th of 1955?

A: Did you ever read that article in "Reader's Digest?"

Q: I've read a few things about that.

A: Yes, I think that's a pretty factual article. Because I was kind of surprised. I have always shied away from newspaper reporters or anything like that, because they're going to structure the thing to make it sound exciting and wild and wooly when it's down to earth work. But Vensel talked to us about it — did we want to talk to these "Reader's Digest" people. We said yes. And after the guy came out and he interviewed us and talked to all of us he wrote his article. Then the people from "Reader's Digest" called and went through it with you.

Q: Oh.

A: Did he say this? Did you say that? Then what happened — they were verifying every line almost in the thing, which I thought was pretty good because it gave you a chance to make some corrections. But I thought it was a pretty interesting day. It was our second flight on the X-1A. We just had inherited it from the Air Force, and we also inherited the other B-29. The B-29's were cut a little differently to carry the different research airplanes. The X-1 B-29 did not carry the Skyrockets and vice versa. But that was a pretty routine flight up until one minute to [launch]. The engineers wanted each of the different rocket airplanes dropped in a different place. I don't really remember why. I remember that the Skyrocket #145 they wanted dropped somewhere west of Rosamond. And the #144 was back out over Lake Elizabeth. The X-1 they wanted dropped clear over by Victorville. So we went out somewhere over Big Bear Lake, in that area. In those days it was interesting. Because in the B-29, I called all the shots. Fire trucks would not go out onto the lake until I called them because we spent the first hour climbing. So after about 20 or 30 minutes of climbing I'd call for the fire trucks to come out. A few minutes later I'd call for the chase airplanes to come on up and join us. I'd set the timing and the whole thing. We didn't have a control room like we have

The TCP test stand. During the 1950s, four rocket powered aircraft suffered explosions - the X-1D, the X-1 #3, the X-2 #2, and the X-1A. Although possible causes for the explosions were suggested, not until the loss of the X-1A did the actual reason surface. Examination of the wreckage revealed traces of tricresyl phosphate (TCP) in the liquid oxygen (lox) tank. All of the rocket aircraft that exploded used leather gaskets treated with TCP. The TCP separated from the leather and pooled in the tanks. At low temperatures TCP exploded under relatively low impact forces, such as when the LOX tank was pressurized. The test stand shown here – designed by NACA engineer Donald Bellman – dropped a five-pound weight ten feet, onto a lox-soaked leather gasket and frozen TCP. In 30 tries, the TCP exploded 30 times. Reexamination of the other explosions supported the leather gasket theory. The accident board concluded that the X-1A had been destroyed by the exploding gaskets, and surmised that this also caused the other three explosions. The gaskets were removed from the remaining rocket aircraft, and no other explosions occurred. (E55-1985)

now. We had nothing really, just a radio that you listened to. I would pick a six minute point out where I wanted to drop. I'd fly two minutes out, and two minutes in the turn, and two minutes back. Somewhere from about ten minutes on down the checklist stuff got pretty busy. I'd call the minutes and Joe would go through what was there for ten minutes, and six minutes, and on down. The procedure was that at one minute Joe's job on his checklist was to pressurize the tanks. And it built pretty good sized pressure. When he flipped the switch it opens the valve and boom — the pressure hits right now in the tanks. For years we'd been doing it like this. But when he flipped the switch it went bang — and there was a tremendous explosion.

I'd usually let the co-pilot do the flying, and I'd kind of turn around and wonder what was going on with the flight engineer and with the co-pilot and the people working with the rocket airplane in the back. When it exploded, I really thought we'd hit another airplane because the B-29 lurched so. But almost immediately I had a call from the F-86 pilot, and he says, "Hey, you've had a fire. There's a fire." Then almost immediately after that he said, "Well, the fire's gone out." Well, you can imagine at 31,000-32,000 feet there's not enough oxygen to support much of a fire, so whatever was burning was just a few seconds. But there's a closeout hole on the back of the liquid oxygen tank — maybe 12-15 inches wide — where they can get in and inspect that it's the closeout after they've manufactured the thing. That is fastened to the tank

Volume 1, Issue 40   NACA HSFS, Edwards, California   October 19, 1956

LITTLETON, MOISE RECEIVE HIGHEST NACA AWARD

Two HSFS employees, Charles W. Littleton and John W. Moise, returned today from Washington, D. C., where they received the NACA's highest honor, the Distinguished Service Medal.

The honor, which consists of a gold medal, a gold lapel emblem, and a citation signed by the Director, has been presented only once previously.

The awards, conferred at a meeting of the Committee at NACA Headquarters, were made "for outstanding bravery beyond the call of duty" following a high-altitude explosion in the rocket-propelled X-1A airplane which endangered three airplanes and the lives of ten men.

Additional recognition will be given by the NACA to seven other HSFS employees and to an Air Force escort pilot, all of whom were involved in the mishap. The honors will be conferred in ceremonies to be conducted at HSFS.

Littleton and Moise were crew members on the B-29 mother airplane which was carrying the research airplane when the August 8, 1955, incident occurred. They are credited with taking action which may have saved the life of the X-1A pilot, Joseph A. Walker.

A few seconds after the X-1A explosion, which took place during a launching operation only 70 seconds before the research airplane was to be dropped, Moise and Littleton rushed to Walker's rescue. Although they were aware that further explosions or fires might follow, they took precarious positions in the B-29 bomb bay in order to open the X-1A canopy and assist Walker from the research airplane. The research airplane was carried to lower altitudes but subsequently had to be released. It was destroyed when it crashed on the desert.

The citations accompanying the Distinguished Service Medals state, "Moise and Littleton risked their lives under extremely hazardous conditions to save the life of a fellow employee."

Chosen to receive the Exceptional Service Award are Walker, X-1A pilot, Stanley P. Butchart, pilot of the B-29, and Richard E. Payne, X-1A crew chief.

Letters of commendation will be presented to John B. McKay, co-pilot of the mother plane, Rex L. Cook, Richard A. DeMore, and Merle C. Woods, B-29 crew members.

Major Arthur Murray, Air Force pilot who was flying a jet "chase" plane, has been commended by Dr. J. C. Hunsaker, NACA Chairman, in a letter to the Secretary of the Air Force. Although his plane was damaged by debris from the explosion, Major Murray continued at his post, giving valuable assistance to the NACA crew.

(Photos on page 3)

From the pages of the X-Press.

with a whole series of bolts, and in between there's a gasket. We always referred to it as an Ulmer gasket. The gasket felt kind of waxy — and you can't use any oils around oxygen at all. So it had to be something that did not have oil in it.

It turned out that this was the fourth accident that happened in a similar way. They lost the X-1D in August of '51 with an explosion after they had aborted the flight and were down at low altitude. The pilot was pressurizing the tanks so he could jettison the fuels and it blew. Anyway, the pilot jumped up and got back into the B-29, and then they dropped it onto the desert right over there by 120th Street. They went through a full lengthy investigation on that and came to some conclusion. A few months later the X-1 number three went through a similar thing where they had aborted a flight, came back down on the ground, to the east end of the field to sit there and go through the jettison process. When he switched to pressurize it blew. Then the X-2 back at Lake Ontario a few years later was in a similar process. All of them had big investigations, and they thought they had come to some conclusion of what was causing it. There was the nitrogen that you carried. In one of the airplanes there was a lot of small tubes, a whole rack of them. They were right behind the pilot, and they were right in front of the liquid oxygen tanks. They were cold. And they felt that the metal got extra brittle and caused the blowing. It wasn't until after the X-1A that Don Bellman, who was one of the instrumental people, did a chemical analysis and found out there were small traces of TCP [tricresyl phosphate] in the cylinder gasket.

Q: What's TCP?

A: It was a chemical, in those days you used to hear of them adding it to Shell gasoline. That would give it more zip....I remember that Shell used to advertise they had TCP in their gas. Bellman found out that small traces of TCP in the presence of oxygen was impact sensitive. So when you pressurized the tank you had quite a jar to it and it blew. Now why it didn't the other few hundred times that they did this process I don't know. But it did on a few occasions. He took us out there on the ramp and showed us a little cup with a steel rod going to it. And in the cup he would put some liquid oxygen and a couple of drops of TCP and then slide a weight down that rod so it would hit there and boom — it just — bang.

Q: So when that explosion occurred on the X-1A, what did you do at that time?

A: Well, things happened pretty fast, and it takes a second or two to assess what in the world has happened. Then when the chase plane calls and you know they have fire — and a lot of people knew that — we had three guys right behind me that helped put Joe in the cockpit and get him out and all. I think they went out there immediately and they were able to get the canopy off. Joe was kind of stunned, I think, when it first happened. Because it was a pretty hard bang in the X-1A itself. It sheared the bolts on a side structure that has pins that go into the X-1A wing. So you knew there was a pretty good load in there. They got into the bomb bay and got the canopy off, and got Joe out. And of course he was unhooked from his oxygen mask the moment he came out. He crawled up forward on the floor beside me. I looked around real quick to try to find an oxygen hose. So I think I used mine momentarily to let him get a couple of breaths of oxygen. Then we located another oxygen hose and got it on him. But he looked like a little lost puppy dog when he came crawling up front there.

Q: So did you have trouble taking the plane in?

A: No, no trouble with it. The thing flew alright. It takes you about, I don't know, 30 minutes or so to get down from altitude. It isn't like a fighter that you can dive down.

An F-100 with the modified taller tail on the Rogers dry lakebed. Butchart and Crossfield both made important contributions to the inertial coupling tests. (This is the same aircraft that Crossfield put into the hangar wall.) (E55-2097)

So we were circling the base and discussing with the ground people. I wanted to land the B-29. It blew the landing gear of the X-1A down also. It unlatched them and they came down. Since they're just a one shot deal when you get ready to land, there's no way to retract them. I thought if we land gently the gears are going to retract some anyway when we land. I thought we could work it that way. But they convinced me that it wasn't a good idea. So the Air Force told me to take it out over PB-6 [bombing range] and drop the X-1A, which was a sad way to get rid of an airplane.

Q: Were you involved in the testing of the F-100A?

A: Yes, I did a lot of work on the A.

Q: Do you remember what year that was?

A: It started in — let's see, we got the F-100 in '54 after we moved up to the new hangars. And it was down for about a year getting instrumented. I guess we started flying it in '55 and I got on it, a few months after it got going. That was probably '55 or '56.

Q: I see. So they were coming up with some kind of redesign because of some accidents?

A: Yes. George Welch was killed in one of the early F-100s. He was a North American pilot, and he was demonstrating the corner of the envelope, a high speed, high-G pullout. When he did, the airplane lost directional control and went sideways. I think the nose broke off. But anyway I don't believe he ejected. But his parachute did open. We had the only instrumented airplane at the time. So North American built a larger tail — I think it was a 10% larger tail vertical — and put it on our airplane and we did the testing of that. It proved that was what they needed. All of them after that had a larger tail vertical.

Q: So what was it like to fly this plane? What were you trying to understand from your work with it?

A: An awful lot of the work that I did in the F-100 was aileron rolls. I did three or four hundred of them. The thing we were trying to hone in on at that time was the early airplane had a very sensitive lateral [throw]. As I remember, the lateral throw was only something like two inches each way and with 30 degrees of aileron. So later on the throw was, I think, four inches each way. But we went through the whole program where we had a pin fastened to the stick. Then a strap was fastened to the side of the cockpit with a piece of metal that had holes in it that gave you two, four, six, eight degrees of aileron. You'd go through a whole series of maneuvers where you'd put it in pin for ten degrees and pop the stick over and get the rolls. You had to do this at two or three different altitudes, then six degrees, and two degrees and on down, trying to see how much they could lower the 30 degrees and still have a moveable airplane.

Q: Were you involved in the large aircraft studies at Dryden with the KC-135?

A: Yes. I did nearly all of the big airplane work at NASA — the B-29's, the B-47 — then I got the KC-135 program in '58. We only had the airplane for three months and we really had to do some fast work. We went two or three times a week with that.

Q: Why were you chosen to fly the big planes?

A photo of the KC-135 and its crew. Butchart served as the project pilot, and conducted tests of new air traffic procedures for the faster and higher flying jet airliners. Left to right: Jack McKay, Stan Butchart, Cecil Dome, Wilber McClenaghan, unknown, Milt Thompson, Bill Betts, Larry Barnett, Don Hall, Captain Bill Lake (USAF) (E58-3914)

A: I liked them. After I got into the B-29's and I was kind of the sole driver of them for four or five years. Then I had the B-47 for about four years. I just kind of fell to it. I liked the big airplanes. Some of the guys thought they were nothing but fighter pilots and wanted to stick with the little ones.

But I had an interesting flight in the KC-135 back on December 11 of '57. It was my [third] checkout flight in the Air Force. There was an Air Force Captain named Bill Lake. He and I were getting checked out in the thing. We took off at about 2:00 in the afternoon. There was a T-33 that took off either right ahead of us or right behind us — I don't remember. And an hour later we met him over Rosamond Lake head on. We weren't at high speed or that at all. We were just moseying along. At the particular time I was not flying. I had gotten out and was standing between the two pilots. I was going through some emergency procedures orally with the Major that was checking us out. He was asking, "What would you do if you lost your fuel pump in that number four tank over there?" I said, "Well, you go from that valve and gravity feed the fuel into the fuselage tank, and you resort to things like that." I was kind of leaning on the two seats looking out the window casually, and all of a sudden I saw this dot out in front of me. The dot got big fast, and all I had time to do was point and open my mouth. I never had time to yell. Fortunately, the Captain that was flying the left seat saw it about the same time I did, and he just jerked on the wheel and all it did was lift our nose up. He hit us in the belly, and he slid through the belly of the tanker for about 40 feet.

It was fortunate the way he hit. Because if he had been off one side or the other, he'd have probably stuck a tip tank down one of our engines. He was only — as I remember — something like nine degrees off our opposite heading, and 14 inches off the center line. He was that close to being in line. It looked like he was coming right into the windshield when I saw him. The Major that was talking to me was looking at me at the time. He said, "What the hell is that?" I said, "We hit another airplane." And he said, "What?" He couldn't believe it. He said, "What was it?" I said, "I think it was a T-33." Well, things got interesting then because we lost cabin pressurization and ruptured some of the structure in the back of the airplane. But being at 20,000 [feet] it isn't as critical as being like 30,000 or 40,000 feet. But I reached down and grabbed the hard hats for the other two guys and my own and put them on.

I turned around and looked in the back. I don't know if you've ever seen a KC-135, but there's nothing in there. It's just like a big tube all the way to the back. There's no seats or anything. I looked at the back and it looked like smoke back at the very rear end, and I thought, "boy, we've got something going." So I went on back to the rear end, and there was a couple of Air Force young fellows that had just bummed a ride with us. They were sitting on the jump seat along the side, and they were white as that cat's white fur. They asked what happened, so I told them the best I knew. I went back and looked and it wasn't smoke. It was JP-4 fumes. The fumes was fogging and filling the thing. And what had happened — I found out later — there was a big hole in the back of the fuselage where this big fuselage tank is that the KC has. We were dumping fuel into it from the wing tank, and it was running out. It went along the fuselage and it also cracked open the refueler dome, where the crewman lays down for the refueling. The JP-4 was seeping in there and foaming as it did. So up front they started to pull the circuit breakers to kill everything in the back of the airplane. Because there was oxygen masks and hoses and everything laying down in there.

But it got interesting, because [the collision] knocked out all our hydraulics. The KC-135 had just two hydraulic pumps on the number two and three engine, and it was a crossover system that was mounted on the forward bulkhead of the wheel well. The T-33 went right through there, and took all that out. So we lost all hydraulics. But fortunately the KC-135, like the 707, had a little feeler aileron that was cable-connected to the wheel just to give the pilot the feel for aileron loading.

That worked alright for us. But it took us about an hour to get down. We had to come down real slow. We had to eventually crank the gear down, and crank the flaps down, and lock out all our radios also. So we couldn't communicate with anybody. But we did turn on the emergency IFF switch. Edwards had a radar in those days that was located out north of Boron, I think. They called Edwards and said, "Hey, we see an emergency IFF out over Rosamond." They got a call about the same time that there was a crash out on Rosamond Dry Lake. So they sent the fire trucks and everything out to Rosamond, thinking that that was where the IFF was coming from, and found that that was a burning heap. Then they called back and said, "Hey, we still see that IFF."

So they sent up an F-100 as a chase plane. He couldn't stay with us — he went by it pretty fast and couldn't slow down because we were getting down pretty low in speed at that time going down. Then they sent up a T-33, and he could sit alongside of us pretty good. I was writing notes to him on a piece of paper — "no hydraulics" — he nodded his head, and I wrote "no brakes" — and he nodded his head. Then when we got down low we saw they had the fire trucks lined up on the main concrete runway — the big one. We couldn't land on that, we wanted the lakebed. So I wrote to him, "the south lakebed." So all the fire trucks moved out to the south lakebed. When we got ready to lower the gear and the flaps, I went back and got these two young Air Force guys to do the cranking. One of them was a six foot something kid — great big feet. When we went to put the gear down, I remembered the emergency instructions, well, they were written on the side of the fuselage in there anyway. He turned the cranks three turns one direction to release the up locks. Then the gear supposedly free fall, and then you could turn it six turns the other way to lock it. The next morning when I looked at the airplane, I wondered why it came down at all because of the shambles through there. But it came down just like the book said. They locked and got a green light, and then we started the flaps down. We really needed to get the flaps at least to 30 degrees. Because when you got past 30 degrees, it brought some outboard ailerons into play.

So I put these young kids to work. The kid put the crank in the hole for the flaps. He started turning and I went to both sides of the airplane to make certain that both flaps were coming down, and nothing happened. I looked back and I told him to try that again, and still nothing happened. Finally, he stood up, and he took his foot and went boom — and he popped that crank down into the hole a little further and away it went. But you had to turn that thing 400 times, I think it was, to get the flaps all the way down. We never did get them all the way down. The air load got too much and you just didn't achieve it. But we got them down far enough to get the ailerons into play. We just landed on the lakebed and we had no nose wheel steering, no brakes, just let her roll.

Q: Wow.

A: And we rolled about three miles I think.

Q: Were you involved in any other accident situations that you recall?

A: Yes. There was another one with a B-29. Neil was my co-pilot that day.

Q: Neil Armstrong?

A: Yes. That was on March 22 of 1956, and it was in the B-29 (modified and designated P2B-1S) and the Skyrocket. Jack McKay was in the Skyrocket. Again, I had gone through the routine of calling for the fire trucks to come onto the lake and then the chase plane. We just about got to our altitude, and I usually worked to get to 31,000-32,000 feet, whichever came easy that day. Sometimes you could get to 34,000, I remember. We just got to altitude and the flight engineer called me and he said, "Hey, number four quit." I said, "What do you mean?" And he said, "It just quit." And I said, "Have you tried cross-feeding the fuel from another tank?" "Yes." "Have you tried..." — I asked him two or three other things. "Yes." He had tried everything. So I wasn't too concerned about it. B-29 engines are not all that dependable anyway. We pushed them hard, you know.

We went at max flying power for about an hour and maybe an hour and a half sometimes to get up there. So I thought — well, no problem — we'll feather the thing. We've done that before. And then go about our business. I pushed the feathering button and it went down to what looked like a feather position and the RPM looked like it had gone to zero. All of a sudden, it started to unfeather from the air loads on it. It hadn't

B-29 LOSES PROPELLER BUT LANDS SAFELY

A safe landing on the Dry Lake was made with the HSFS B-29 late yesterday after one of its propellers tore loose and ripped into the fuselage of the four-engine bomber. The accident occurred 30,000 feet over Palmdale while the B-29 was preparing to launch the Douglas D-558-II (144) Skyrocket.

According to crew members, when an intense vibration was suddenly felt from the No. 4 engine, Pilot Stanley P. Butchart immediately nosed the B-29 downward and cut loose the 144, piloted by John B. McKay. McKay jettisoned his rocket propellants and glided to a safe landing on the Lake.

Almost as soon as the Skyrocket had cast off, the propeller pulled loose from the bomber's No. 4 engine, ripped up the nacelle of the No. 3 engine, then plunged through the bomb bay and crashed out the other side of the fuselage.

Because the pilot's aileron control cables were cut by the propeller, it was necessary for Co-pilot Neil H. Armstrong to bring the bomber home.

None of the seven men aboard the B-29 was injured. Crew members on the flight were:
Pilot - Butchart
Co-pilot - Armstrong
Engineer - Joseph L. Tipton
Scanners - Lester. H. Booth
Norman K. Jones
Crew (144) - Homer H. Hall
Thomas J. Raczkowski

Flying chase for the flight were Air Force captains Loren W. Davis and Iven C. Kinchloe.

A committee, composed of the following HSFS personnel, was appointed today by Walter C. Williams, Chief of the Station, to investigate the accident:
Chairman-Donald R. Bellman
Kenneth S. Kleinknecht
Joseph A. Walker

From the pages of the X-Press.

Stan Butchart had many close calls during his years as a research pilot. One of these involved the near loss of the P2B drop plane (the Navy designation for the B-29) in March 1956. After an in flight engine failure, Butchart tried to feather the number four propeller. But due to the airplane's high speed, the propeller rotated so fast that it broke apart, throwing debris into the number 3 engine and fuselage. Pilot John McKay and the D-558-II were dropped from the P2B only moments before the propeller disintegrated. McKay jettisoned the Skyrocket's propellant and glided it to a successful landing on the lakebed. The P2B required extensive repairs, and it did not make another launch until August 24, 1956.

gone quite far enough, so that the air loads on the blade was pushing it to unfeather. As it unfeathered, the RPM's started up. And I thought — boy, we've got it now. I thought about it a minute and then I decided well — maybe if I push that button and hold it real hard it will get it feathered all the way.

Well, all it did was get to the end of the button top with my finger still on it, so I pushed it and then it was in the unfeather position for the second time I pushed it. So I gave up on that. I could just to this day picture in the handbook one page in there where it told about if you had a runaway propeller, and you were above 20,000 feet, and you couldn't get it slowed down below, I think, 120 [knots], that you were going to have a centrifugal disintegration. Just put it at a slower speed and go. I could see that page real clear. So about that time, Jack called because we were already into our six minute pattern. All this was going on, Neil was doing the flying, and I was directing where we wanted to go. Jack calls and says, "Hey, Butch — you can't drop me. My Grover loader valve just broke." It was a valve that was down by the side that you used to build up the pressure on one of his systems. I don't remember which one.

But he said he felt the valve pop in his hand on the shaft. I guess he couldn't go up any higher on the pressure. Well, the other thing is, our B-29's had only enough oil for three feather cycles. For practice you could feather and unfeather and then you had one more for real. I had already gone through two of them. So I knew I had one more. I thought well, I'll give it one more try.

So I pushed it again. It went down and almost fully feathered again, and looked like it was going to stop. Then it started unwinding and away it went. I knew at that time that we were in deep trouble. So I told Neil, and I called Jack and I said, "Jack, I've got to drop you." I motioned to Neil to nose over because you usually had to put the B-29 in a slight dive to get up to the drop speed so that the Skyrocket wouldn't come out in a stall. Get him up over 200, so Neil did. And when he got up to 200, the speed we were looking for, I reached up and grabbed the emergency release which I had never used. But I knew it was there all the time. I gave that a pull and nothing happened. I pulled it two or three times real quick. Then I reached up and you have two switches you have to throw on the dash, plus the pickle button. I threw those two switches and pickled Jack off, and he dropped.

It seemed like it was only about 10-15 seconds after that that the engine went kaboom. It was a centrifugal disintegration, and parts just went in all four directions. In fact, Neil said that the big nose bullet on the propeller went by him. We were probably doing 300 or 400 [knots] true air speed. One of the air blades came off through the air induction scoop on the bottom of the number three engine, went through the bomb bay, and hit my number two engine. So it was going at a good clip.

After it was over with, everything is quiet. I thought — whew, we're home free. Then I turned around, and I went to take over control again. And the wheel was completely loose on my side — nothing. The aileron was gone. I looked over and Neil was still hanging on. And I said, "Do you have lateral control?" He said, "Yes, a little bit." He had some slop in the wheel but he picked up the catch. So between the two of us we got the thing down. Of course we were at 30,000 feet, so we just kind of made a long glide out past Boron, back in, and made it straight in on the north lakebed. But once we got down we saw what the problem was. It had cut my aileron cables completely, and it had slashed his aileron cable down to where he had about one or two strands left. When you cut a cable under tension like that it frays out, and that fraying was catching in one of the fairleads. That was what was catching every once in awhile.

Q: Of all the planes you've flown, which is your best memory? In other words, what project did you most enjoy taking part in?

A: Oh, I've been asked that before. And I think I keep coming back to the B-47. It was a fun airplane and it was pretty advanced for its day. I just enjoyed flying it. It's also interesting that when Scott and I were going to the University of Washington, we had a professor that had come from Boeing in '47 I think. We took aircraft structures from him. But he had worked for Boeing, and he had been the design engineer on the B-47 wing. So you felt like he had some personal knowledge of how the whole thing developed back in the early days. But it was a nice airplane to fly. It was tricky too, you know, with the little bicycle landing gear. You had to be down to just the right speed so you touched front and rear at the same time. If you were shooting touch and go's, your co-pilot would keep checking your weight. And maybe every time you'd have to reduce your air speed a little bit. You had to keep it low. If you get too fast and you touch the first one front gear down, then it had a tendency to porpoise. If you touched the back one down, it could put too much of a load on the front gear. But if you had the speed down right it just touched down nice.

Q: Can you describe how, as technology evolved, the work and life at the Flight

Research Center changed? In other words, how did technology change the life and work you did out there?

A: Well, I think the technology evolved kind of with the speed in which we were advancing airplanes. Particularly I think of the recording systems that we had. Early on, like I said, we had no radar. All we had was a guy sitting in a room talking to you. Then later on we had a very simple plotting board that gave you an XY plot of where the flight was. Then, of course, when the X-15 came along, we started developing that control room upstairs which was just very simple to start with. There was no radar plot display on the wall. It was just dials in front of you. I think the technology and that sort of stuff was as big a boon to the pilots as it was to the gathering of the data. You had somebody to help you look over the gauges and watch to see what was going on.

Q: You were a contributor to several research papers while you worked at —

A: Well, the only one that comes to mind mainly was the work on the KC-135. And that was all aimed at looking at the KC-135 as a civilian transport. It was basically the same airplane as a 707. The airlines were going to introduce the 707s in the fall of '58. I think American [Airlines] got the first ones. And there was a lot of discussion about how they were going to fit in with traffic — how the pilots were going to be able to transition to them from props, and deal with the different flight characteristics of a swept-wing airplane. So we used the KC-135 as a civilian transport in the work we did with it. The papers that were given that fall back at Langley — I gave one and Jack Fischel gave the other one. He gave a talk on the low speed end of it and the handling qualities. I gave the paper on the high speed end of it. Of course it was to a lot of the airline representatives there.

Q: What type of aviation activities have you been involved with since your retirement — any at all?

A: Nothing other than keeping up my activity and my active participation in our Test Pilot's Society. I was a charter member in the Society when we started in '55. We finally got chartered in '56. There were 65 of us that were charter members, and now there's about 1,800 or so. They're all over the world. We've even got Russian pilots in now. It grew from just a handful of us starting. I think there were five fellows who went to lunch one day back in '55 and talked about it. This one fellow had a vision of what he wanted that was — what it was going to be like to form this Society. The next week a few more of us joined in. Then word got out and we had probably at least 65. We spent almost a year having a dinner every Thursday night, and then assigning sections of the Constitution to different people to write up. It took us about a year to put the whole thing together. But it's become a very worldwide prestigious organization.

Q: Looking back at your career, what are the main research contributions that you have been involved in? And what major technical innovations resulted from projects you worked on?

A: I don't really know. I think a lot of the work we did in those early days was pitch up's. It was a problem — it was a very serious problem with the airplanes. And we tried to find ways to alleviate it or to live with it. And that was the work I did on the X-5, that's what I did on the F-100, on the F-86.... it was 36 years of flying. And it was all interesting, up to the last.

Epilogue

The early years of the NACA's High Speed Flight Station concluded with the demise of the NACA itself. The era ended for several reasons. By the early 1960s, Mach 2 performance had become the norm for fighter aircraft, and – from a military viewpoint – not much could be gained by increasing speeds further. Also, during most of the 1950s, one generation of aircraft succeeded another by only a few years. By the end of the decade, this pattern changed. The fighter aircraft introduced during the late 1950s continued in service for a decade, and not until the mid-1970s did a whole new generation of fighters appear.

But as one frontier closed, another opened. This change involved a landmark event in human history. On October 4, 1957, the Soviet Union launched Sputnik 1, the first artificial satellite, an event deeply troubling to the American people. Spaceflight - an idea that many scientists had dismissed as fit only for *Tom Corbett: Space Cadet* or other children's television shows — suddenly became part of the rivalry between the U.S. and the Soviet Union.

As a result of Sputnik's launch, the NACA became the core of a new organization: the National Aeronautics and Space Administration (NASA). The change-over became official on October 1, 1958. Less than a year later, on September 27, 1959, the High-Speed Flight Station became the NASA Flight Research Center. The new emphasis on space became clear. In 1955, research attention focused on such issues as inertial coupling, roll rates for Mach 2 fighters, and transonic airloads and drag. By 1958, emphasis had shifted to hypersonic boost-gliders, reaction controls, satellites, and winged spacecraft. The amount of time devoted to space-related activities increased by two or three, while research on aircraft technology dropped by that much or more.

The X-15 represented the signature space activity of the Flight Research Center during the 1960s. Conceived during the mid-1950s, this aircraft carried the nation into the space age, flying as fast as Mach 6.7 and achieving altitudes above 50 miles, the realm of space. The X-15 stimulated another transformation of the Flight Research Center; most of the facility's personnel now supported the X-15 program. Moreover, by its final flight in 1968, the X-15 had provided data and experience critical to the design of the space shuttle.

Even as the X-15 set new altitude and speed records in the early 1960s, other space-related activities began. The Lunar Landing Research Vehicle (LLRV) proved the feasibility of a soft landing on the Moon. Additionally, the lifting body program tested a variety of new configurations, much as the X-3, X-4, and X-5 had a decade before. In concept, the lifting bodies continued the local initiative and can-do spirit of the early days at South Base. Dale Reed conducted his initial tests with models, flown down the hallways of the main building, launched off its roof, and carried aloft by remote controlled model airplanes. Construction of a full-scale prototype cost surprisingly little. Built in the corner of a hangar, the M2-F1's exterior was made of wood and its internal framework consisted of welded steel tubing. For the next decade, the heavy-weight lifting bodies — the M2-F2, M2-F3, HL-10, and X-24A/B — tested different configurations. Although the shuttle design ultimately had wings, the lifting bodies (as well as the X-15) gave confidence that the Shuttle Orbiter could re-enter from space and make a safe landing on a runway.

Sources

Air Force Flight Test Center History Office, *Edwards Then And Now* (2001).

Day, Richard E. "Coupled Dynamics in Aircraft: A Historical Prospective," NASA Special Publication 532 (Edwards, California: Dryden Flight Research Center, 1997).

Gorn, Michael H., *Expanding The Envelope Flight Research At NACA And NASA* (Lexington, Kentucky: University Press of Kentucky, 2001).

Hallion, Richard P., and Michael Gorn, *On The Frontier Experimental Flight at NASA Dryden, 1946-2000* (Washington D.C.: Smithsonian Institution Press 2003).

Powers, Sheryll Goecke "Woman in Flight Research at NASA Dryden Flight Research Center from 1946 to 1995" (Edwards, California: Dryden Flight Research Center, 1997).

Starr, Kevin, *Embattled Dreams California In War And Peace 1940-1950* (New York: Oxford University Press, 2002).

About The Author

Curtis Peebles has been working at the NASA Dryden Flight Research Center since November 2000. He is employed by Analytical Services & Materials, Inc. A freelance writer since 1977, he has written 11 books, including *Dark Eagles, The Corona Project, Flying Without Wings* (with the late NASA research pilot Milt Thompson), and *Asteroids: A History*, as well as more than forty articles on various aspects of Cold War aerospace history. He received a BA in History from Cal State University Long Beach in 1985. Peebles is a Fellow of the British Interplanetary Society and a member of the Flight Test Historical Foundation.

Acknowledgments

I want to first thank the individuals who's observations, opinions, and recollections appear in this monograph, and for their willingness to share them. While documents and official records record events, only recollections such as these can let us know what it was actually like to be there when those events happened. Thanks also to Betty Love, who contributed one of the accounts. She is an ex-computer who now works as a volunteer at the Dryden history office, providing fifty years of living history. Thanks also to Rick Norwood, the Edwards AFB archeologist, for the Air Force interview of Walt Williams; to Jay Levine for scanning the Richard Day interview; the Dryden photo lab for scanning the images used in the monograph; to Dr. Michael Gorn, Peter Merlin, and Dr. Christian Gelzer for proofreading and fact-checking; and to Steve Lighthill for his imaginative book design and page layout.

Index

Aircraft, research.
  B-24, 48.
  B-29/P2B, 4, 8, 80, 91, 101, 112, 114-119, 121-123.
  B-47, 28, 31, 101, 114, 119, 123.
  C-46, 48.
  C-82, 48.
  D-558-I, 3, 4, 39, 40, 47, 49, 50, 80, 84, 90, 91, 101, 106, 107, 112, 113.
  D-558-II, 4, 5, 8, 44, 47, 50, 51, 59, 77, 79, 80, 84, 87, 91-93, 98, 101, 107, 112-114, 121-123.
  F7U, 52, 53, 79.
  F-84, 107, 108, 112.
  F-100A, 63, 64, 67, 69-71, 77, 83-85, 93, 94, 118, 119, 124.
  F-104, 74.
  JF-107A, 64, 93-95.
  KC-135, 94-96, 101, 119-121, 124.
  Lifting Bodies, 125.
  Lunar Landing Research Vehicle (LLRV), 125.
  P-51, 45, 46, 112.
  U-2, 66.
  X-1, 3-5, 7, 25, 34, 43, 47, 49, 50, 52, 67, 77, 80, 81, 92, 108.
  X-1A, 57, 114-118.
  X-1B, 74.
  X-2, 5, 53, 68, 71-73, 84, 92.
  X-3, 5, 60, 64, 67-70, 87, 92, 93, 94.
  X-4, 4, 5, 28, 39, 40, 43, 47, 51, 77, 79, 92, 101, 107, 112, 113.
  X-5, 4, 5, 59, 77, 81, 92, 101, 107, 112, 113, 124.
  X-15, 59, 64, 72, 77, 84, 85, 93, 94, 125.
  XB-70, 59.
  XF-92A, 4, 5, 67, 77, 81, 82.
  YB-49A, 5.
Antelope Valley Fair and Alfalfa Festival, 39.
Apt, Capt. Milburn, 53, 71-73, 84, 111.
Armstrong, Neil, 34, 61, 108, 109, 121-123.
Aviation Writers Association, 12, 13.

Bailey, Clyde, 18-46, 81.
Barnes, Florence "Pancho," 2, 6, 9-16, 38, 43.
Beeler, De, 33, 38, 45, 49, 57, 59, 60, 69, 90, 96.
Bikle, Paul, 16, 60, 61, 70, 96, 97, 111.
Borchers, Don, 18-46.
Boyd, Col. Albert, 10, 11, 13, 64.
Buffet, vibration, and flutter, 59, 60.

Bush, George, 105.
Butchart, Stanley P., 95, 96, 101-124.

Car pools, 91, 92.
Champine, Bob, 47, 49, 78, 108.
Chance Vought Aircraft, 47, 52, 53.
Clark, J. R., 52.
Computers (electronic), 59, 67, 69, 71-74, 77.
Computers (human), 4, 39, 55-61, 91.
Cox, Richard, 18-46.
Crash research, 48.
Crossfield, A. Scott, 43, 44, 50, 77-86, 101, 104, 105, 108, 109, 112, 113, 118, 123.

Dampers, 68, 70, 71.
Dana, Bill, 94, 109.
Day, Richard E., 67-75, 93.
Drake, Hubert, 49, 53, 69, 70, 84, 90.
Dryden, Hugh L., 10, 66.
Duntley Ranch, 29.

Edwards, Capt. Glen, 5.
Escape capsules, 84, 85, 110.
Everest, Lt. Col. Pete, 64, 72, 80, 82.

Fischel, Jack, 70, 87-99.
Fisken, Tom, 59, 60.
Flight Research Center, 125.
Friden calculator, 58, 59.

Gilkey, Col. Signa, 8-10, 13.
Goodlin, Chalmers "Slick," 10.
Gough, Eddie, 32, 33, 48, 49. 108.
Gough, Mel, 25, 26, 30-32, 49.
Gray, Bill, 45.
Griffith, John, 33, 43, 47-53, 78.

Hanna, Dick, 44.
Happy Bottom Riding Club, 2, 6, 9-16, 38, 43.
Harwell, Walter "Rebel," 99.
High-Speed Flight Research Station, 6, 8, 67.
High-Speed Flight Station, 6, 63, 64, 67, 91, 125.
Holtoner, Gen. J. Stanley, 13, 14, 16.
Hoover, Bob, 83.
Hoover, Herb, 43, 49, 108.
Hope, Bob, 43.
Hughes, Howard, 8, 34, 35.

Icing research, 48.
Inertial coupling, 63, 64, 67-73, 77, 87, 92-94.

Instrumentation, 51, 98, 99.

Jensen, George, 112.
"Jet Pilot" (movie), 52.
Jones, Walt, 108, 109, 112.

Kerosene Flats, 2, 6, 9, 21, 55.
Kincheloe, Capt. Iven C., 72.
Knapp, Col. Howard C. 15.

Lake, Capt. Bill, 119-121.
Laminar flow, 45.
Lancaster, 1, 21, 36, 37, 41, 52, 58, 75, 91, 92,
Langley Memorial Aeronautical Laboratory, 1, 3, 19, 20, 25, 26, 31, 42, 49, 69, 87-91, 97, 98.
Lewis Propulsion Laboratory, 47-49, 109.
Lilly, Howard, 43.
Lookout Mountain Air Force Station, 60.
Love, Betty, 55-61.

Ma Greene's café, 25, 43.
Martin, Isabell, 4.
McKay, Jack, 95, 109, 119, 121-123.
Men's Dorm, 22, 24, 56, 64.
Mojave, 1, 9, 20, 21, 29, 30, 37, 74, 90, 91.
Morris, Cliff, 14, 16, 17.
Muroc Flight Test Unit, 4-6.

Officer's club, 23, 25, 26, 28, 29.

Palmdale, 1, 9, 21, 37.
"Pathway to the Stars" (movie), 60.
Payne, Dick, 28, 40.
Phillips, William H., 68, 69, 71.
Pitch up, 50, 64, 87, 92, 93, 98, 113.
Popson, Maj. Ray, 81, 113.
Power, Gen. Thomas S., 84.
Proctor, LeRoy, 25, 30.

Rattlesnakes, 36.
Reaction Control Systems, 53, 74.
Reed, Dale, 125.
Ridley, Jack, 81.

Shoop, Col. Richard R., 9.
Snow, 36, 37, 59.
Soule, Hartley, 32, 33, 89.
Sparks, Ralph, 18-46.
Sports teams, 26, 27, 64, 65, 110, 111.
Sputnik I, 125.
Stack, John, 3, 32, 33.
Starr, Kevin, 1.

Storms, Harrison, 85.
Structures, 59.

Tehachapi, 21.
Thompson, Milt, 101, 109, 119.
Tricresyl phosphate (TCP), 115-117.

United Airlines, 47, 53.

Vensel, Joe, 27, 28, 34, 41, 44, 45, 49, 51, 79, 96, 106, 109, 111, 114.

Walker, Joe, 37, 44, 60, 81, 93, 94, 108, 109, 112, 113, 114, 117.
Weil, Joe, 69, 70, 97, 98.
Welch, George, 63, 64, 118.
Westinghouse, 47, 53.
Wherry housing, 25, 38.
White's Motel, 1, 29, 30.
Williams, Walter C., 4, 7-17, 19, 25, 26, 28, 30, 32, 43, 44, 49, 51, 57, 59-61, 64, 69, 70, 78, 84, 89, 90, 96, 111.
Willow Springs, 28, 29, 40.
Wolfe, Capt. Joe, 114.
Women's Dorm, 55, 56, 64.

XLR-99 rocket engine, 85.
X-Press, 17, 22, 26, 27, 36, 45, 47, 61, 64-66, 70, 72, 73, 86, 99, 108, 116, 122.
Yancey, Roxanah, 4, 39, 55, 58, 59.
Yeager, Capt. Chuck, 5, 10, 33, 38, 57, 108, 109.

Monographs in Aerospace History (SP-4500 Series)

Launius, Roger D. and Aaron K. Gillette, comps. *Toward a History of the Space Shuttle: An Annotated Bibliography.* Monograph in Aerospace History, No. 1, 1992.

Launius, Roger D., and J.D. Hunley, comps. *An Annotated Bibliography of the Apollo Program.* Monograph in Aerospace History No. 2, 1994.

Launius, Roger D. *Apollo: A Retrospective Analysis.* Monograph in Aerospace History, No. 3, 1994.

Hansen, James R. *Enchanted Rendezvous: John C. Houbolt and the Genesis of the Lunar-Orbit Rendezvous Concept.* Monograph in Aerospace History, No. 4, 1995.

Gorn, Michael H. *Hugh L. Dryden's Career in Aviation and Space.* Monograph in Aerospace History, No. 5, 1996.

Powers, Sheryll Goecke. *Women in Flight Research at NASA Dryden Flight Research Center from 1946 to 1995.* Monograph in Aerospace History, No. 6, 1997.

Portree, David S.F. and Robert C. Trevino. *Walking to Olympus: An EVA Chronology.* Monograph in Aerospace History, No. 7, 1997.

Logsdon, John M., moderator. *Legislative Origins of the National Aeronautics and Space Act of 1958: Proceedings of an Oral History Workshop.* Monograph in Aerospace History, No. 8, 1998.

Rumerman, Judy A., comp. *U.S. Human Spaceflight, A Record of Achievement 1961-1998.* Monograph in Aerospace History, No. 9, 1998.

Portree, David S. F. *NASA's Origins and the Dawn of the Space Age.* Monograph in Aerospace History, No. 10, 1998.

Logsdon, John M. *Together in Orbit: The Origins of International Cooperation in the Space Station.* Monograph in Aerospace History, No. 11, 1998.

Phillips, W. Hewitt. *Journey in Aeronautical Research: A Career at NASA Langley Research Center.* Monograph in Aerospace History, No. 12, 1998.

Braslow, Albert L. *A History of Suction-Type Laminar-Flow Control with Emphasis on Flight Research.* Monograph in Aerospace History, No. 13, 1999.

Logsdon, John M., moderator. *Managing the Moon Program: Lessons Learned From Apollo.* Monograph in Aerospace History, No. 14, 1999.

Perminov, V.G. *The Difficult Road to Mars: A Brief History of Mars Exploration in the Soviet Union.* Monograph in Aerospace History, No. 15, 1999.

Tucker, Tom. *Touchdown: The Development of Propulsion Controlled Aircraft at NASA Dryden.* Monograph in Aerospace History, No. 16, 1999.

Maisel, Martin, Giulanetti, Demo J., and Dugan, Daniel C. *The History of the XV-15 Tilt Rotor Research Aircraft: From Concept to Flight.* Monograph in Aerospace History, No. 17 (NASA SP-2000-4517).

Jenkins, Dennis R., *Hypersonics Before the Shuttle: A Concise History of the X-15 Research Airplane*. Monograph in Aerospace History, No. 18 (NASA SP-2000-4518).

Chambers, Joseph R. *Partners in Freedom: Contributions of the Langley Research Center to U.S. Military Aircraft of the 1990s*. Monograph in Aerospace History, No. 19 (NASA SP-2000-4519).

Waltman, Gene L. *Black Magic and Gremlins: Analog Flight Simulations at NASA's Flight Research Center*. Monograph in Aerospace History, No. 20 (NASA SP-2000-4520).

Portree, David S.F.. *Humans to Mars: Fifty Years of Mission Planning, 1950-2000*. Monograph in Aerospace History, No. 21 (NASA SP-2001-4521).

Thompson, Milton O. with J.D. Hunley. *Flight Research: Problems Encountered and What they Should Teach Us*. Monograph in Aerospace History, No. 22 (NASA SP-2001-4522).

Tucker, Tom. *The Eclipse Project*. Monograph in Aerospace History, No. 23 (NASA SP-2001-4523).

Siddiqi, Asif A. *Deep Space Chronicle: A Chronology of Deep Space and Planetary Probes 1958-2000*. Monograph in Aerospace History, No. 24 (NASA SP-2002-4524).

Merlin, Peter W. *Mach 3+: NASA/USAF YF-12 Flight Research, 1969-1979*. Monograph in Aerospace History, No. 25 (NASA SP-2001-4525).

Anderson, Seth B. *Memoirs of an Aeronautical Engineer, Flight Test at Ames Research Center: 1940-1970*. Monograph in Aerospace History, No. 26 (NASA SP-2002-4526).

Renstrom, Arthur G. *Wilbur and Orville Wright: A Bibliography Commemorating the One-Hundredth Anniversary of the First Powered Flight on December 17, 1903*. Monograph in Aerospace History, No. 27 (NASA SP-2002-4527).

Chambers, Joseph R. *Concept to Reality: Contributions of the Langley Research Center to the U.S. Civil Aircraft of the 1990s*. Monograph in Aerospace History, No. 29 (NASA SP-2002-4529).

Reference Works, NASA SP-4000

Grimwood, James M. *Project Mercury: A Chronology*. NASA SP-4001, 1963.

Grimwood, James M., and Barton C. Hacker, with Peter J. Vorzimmer. *Project Gemini Technology and Operations: A Chronology*. NASA SP-4002, 1969.

Link, Mae Mills. *Space Medicine in Project Mercury*. NASA SP-4003, 1965.

Astronautics and Aeronautics, 1963: Chronology of Science, Technology, and Policy. NASA SP-4004, 1964.

Astronautics and Aeronautics, 1964: Chronology of Science, Technology, and Policy. NASA SP-4005, 1965.

Astronautics and Aeronautics, 1965: Chronology of Science, Technology, and Policy. NASA SP-4006, 1966.

Astronautics and Aeronautics, 1966: Chronology of Science, Technology, and Policy. NASA SP-4007, 1967.

Astronautics and Aeronautics, 1967: Chronology of Science, Technology, and Policy. NASA SP-4008, 1968.

Ertel, Ivan D., and Mary Louise Morse. *The Apollo Spacecraft: A Chronology, Volume I, Through November 7, 1962*. NASA SP-4009, 1969.

Morse, Mary Louise, and Jean Kernahan Bays. *The Apollo Spacecraft: A Chronology, Volume II, November 8, 1962-September 30, 1964*. NASA SP-4009, 1973.

Brooks, Courtney G., and Ivan D. Ertel. *The Apollo Spacecraft: A Chronology, Volume III, October 1, 1964-January 20, 1966*. NASA SP-4009, 1973.

Ertel, Ivan D., and Roland W. Newkirk, with Courtney G. Brooks, *The Apollo Spacecraft: A Chronology, Volume IV, January 21, 1966-July 13, 1974*. NASA SP-4009, 1978.

Astronautics and Aeronautics, 1968: Chronology of Science, Technology, and Policy. NASA SP-4010, 1969.

Newkirk, Roland W., and Ivan D. Ertel, with Courtney G. Brooks, *Skylab: A Chronology*. NASA SP-4011, 1977.

Van Nimmen, Jane, and Leonard C. Bruno, with Robert L. Rosholt. *NASA Historical Data Book, Vol. I: NASA Resources, 1958-1968*. NASA SP-4012, 1976, rep. ed. 1988.

Ezell, Linda Neuman. *NASA Historical Data Book, Vol II: Programs and Projects, 1958-1968*. NASA SP-4012, 1988.

Ezell, Linda Neuman. *NASA Historical Data Book, Vol. III: Programs and Projects, 1969-1978*. NASA SP-4012, 1988.

Gawdiak, Ihor, with Helen Fedor. *NASA Historical Data Book, Vol. IV: NASA Resources, 1969-1978*. NASA SP-4012, 1994.

Rumerman, Judy A. *NASA Historical Data Book, Vol. V: NASA Launch Systems, Space Transportation, Human Spaceflight, and Space Science, 1979-1988*. NASA SP-4012, 1999.

Rumerman, Judy A. *NASA Historical Data Book, Vol. VI: Space Applications, Aeronautics, and other topics, 1979-1988*. NASA SP-4012, 1999.

Astronautics and Aeronautics, 1969: Chronology of Science, Technology, and Policy. NASA SP-4014, 1970.

Astronautics and Aeronautics, 1970: Chronology of Science, Technology, and Policy. NASA SP-4015, 1972.

Astronautics and Aeronautics, 1971: Chronology of Science, Technology, and Policy. NASA SP-4016, 1972.

Astronautics and Aeronautics, 1972: Chronology of Science, Technology, and Policy. NASA SP-4017, 1974.

Astronautics and Aeronautics, 1973: Chronology of Science, Technology, and Policy. NASA SP-4018, 1975.

Astronautics and Aeronautics, 1974: Chronology of Science, Technology, and Policy. NASA SP-4019, 1977.

Astronautics and Aeronautics, 1975: Chronology of Science, Technology, and Policy. NASA SP-4020, 1979.

Astronautics and Aeronautics, 1976: Chronology of Science, Technology, and Policy. NASA SP-4021, 1984.

Astronautics and Aeronautics, 1977: Chronology of Science, Technology, and Policy. NASA SP-4022, 1986.

Astronautics and Aeronautics, 1978: Chronology of Science, Technology, and Policy. NASA SP-4023, 1986.

Astronautics and Aeronautics, 1979-1984: Chronology of Science, Technology, and Policy. NASA SP-4024, 1988.

Astronautics and Aeronautics, 1985: Chronology of Science, Technology, and Policy. NASA SP-4025, 1990.

Noordung, Hermann. *The Problem of Space Travel: The Rocket Motor.* Edited by Ernst Stuhlinger and J.D. Hunley, with Jennifer Garland. NASA SP-4026, 1995.

Gawdiak, Ihor Y., Ramon J. Miro, and Sam Stueland, comps. *Astronautics and Aeronautics, 1986-1990: A Chronology.* NASA SP-4027, 1997.

Gawdiak, Ihor Y. and Shetland, Charles. *Astronautics and Aeronautics, 1990-1995: A Chronology.* NASA SP-2000-4028, 2000.

Orloff, Richard W. *Apollo by the Numbers: A Statistical Reference.* NASA SP-2000-4029, 2000.

Management Histories, NASA SP-4100

Rosholt, Robert L. *An Administrative History of NASA, 1958-1963.* NASA SP-4101,

Levine, Arnold S. *Managing NASA in the Apollo Era.* NASA SP-4102, 1982.

Roland, Alex. *Model Research: The National Advisory Committee for Aeronautics, 1915-1958.* NASA SP-4103, 1985.

Fries, Sylvia D. *NASA Engineers and the Age of Apollo.* NASA SP-4104, 1992.

Glennan, T. Keith. *The Birth of NASA: The Diary of T. Keith Glennan.* Edited by J.D. Hunley. NASA SP-4105, 1993.

Seamans, Robert C. *Aiming at Targets: The Autobiography of Robert C. Seamans.* NASA SP-4106, 1996

Garber, Stephen J., editor. *Looking Backward, Looking Forward: Forty Years of Human Spaceflight Symposium.* NASA SP-2002-4107.

Project Histories, NASA SP-4200

Swenson, Loyd S., Jr., James M. Grimwood, and Charles C. Alexander. *This New Ocean: A History of Project Mercury.* NASA SP-4201, 1966, reprinted 1999.

Green, Constance McLaughlin, and Milton Lomask. *Vanguard: A History.* NASA SP-4202, 1970; rep. ed. Smithsonian Institution Press, 1971

Hacker, Barton C., and James M. Grimwood. *On Shoulders of Titans: A History of Project Gemini.* NASA SP-4203, 1977, reprinted 2002.

Benson, Charles D. and William Barnaby Faherty, *Moonport: A History of Apollo Launch Facilities and Operations.* NASA SP-4204, 1978.

Brooks, Courtney G., James M. Grimwood, and Loyd S. Swenson, Jr. *Chariots for Apollo: A History of Manned Lunar Spacecraft.* NASA SP-4205, 1979.

Bilstein, Roger E. *Stages to Saturn: A Technological History of the Apollo/Saturn Launch Vehicles.* NASA SP-4206, 1980 and 1996.

Compton, W. David, and Charles D. Benson. *Living and Working in Space: A History of Skylab.* NASA SP-4208, 1983.

Ezell, Edward Clinton, and Linda Neuman Ezell. *The Partnership: A History of the Apollo-Soyuz Test Project.* NASA SP-4209, 1978..

Hall, R. Cargill. *Lunar Impact: A History of Project Ranger.* NASA SP-4210, 1977.

Newell, Homer E. *Beyond the Atmosphere: Early Years of Space Science.* NASA SP-4211, 1980.

Ezell, Edward Clinton, and Linda Neuman Ezell. *On Mars: Exploration of the Red Planet, 1958-1978.* NASA SP-4212, 1984.

Pitts, John A. *The Human Factor: Biomedicine in the Manned Space Program to 1980.* NASA SP-4213, 1985.

Compton, W. David. *Where No Man Has Gone Before: A History of Apollo Lunar Exploration Missions.* NASA SP-4214, 1989.

Naugle, John E. *First Among Equals: The Selection of NASA Space Science Experiments* NASA SP-4215, 1991.

Wallace, Lane E. *Airborne Trailblazer: Two Decades with NASA Langley's 737 Flying Laboratory.* NASA SP-4216, 1994.

Butrica, Andrew J. *Beyond the Ionosphere: Fifty Years of Satellite Communications.* NASA SP-4217, 1997.

Butrica, Andrew J. *To See the Unseen: A History of Planetary Radar Astronomy.* NASA SP-4218, 1996.

Mack, Pamela E., ed. *From Engineering Science to Big Science: The NACA and NASA Collier Trophy Research Project Winners.* NASA SP-4219, 1998.

Reed, R. Dale. *Wingless Flight: The Lifting Body Story.* NASA SP-4220, 1998.

Heppenheimer, T. A. *The Space Shuttle Decision: NASA's Search for a Reusable Space Vehicle.* NASA SP-4221, 1999.

Hunley, J. D., ed. *Toward Mach 2: The Douglas D-558 Program.* NASA SP-4222, 1999.

Swanson, Glen E., ed. *"Before This Decade is Out..." Personal Reflections on the Apollo Program.* NASA SP-4223, 1999.

Tomayko, James E. *Computers Take Flight: A History of NASA's Pioneering Digital Fly-By-Wire Project* NASA SP-4224, 2000.

Leary, William M. *We Freeze to Please: A History of NASA's Icing Research Tunnel and the Quest for Safety.* NASA SP-2002-4226, 2002.

Mudgway, Douglas J. *Uplink-Downlink: A History of the Deep Space Network, 1957-1997.* NASA SP-2001-4227.

Center Histories, NASA SP-4300

Rosenthal, Alfred. *Venture into Space: Early Years of Goddard Space Flight Center.* NASA SP-4301, 1985.

Hartman, Edwin, P. *Adventures in Research: A History of Ames Research Center, 1940-1965.* NASA SP-4302, 1970.

Hallion, Richard P. *On the Frontier: Flight Research at Dryden, 1946-1981.* NASA SP-4303, 1984.

Muenger, Elizabeth A. *Searching the Horizon: A History of Ames Research Center, 1940-1976.* NASA SP-4304, 1985.

Hansen, James R. *Engineer in Charge: A History of the Langley Aeronautical Laboratory, 1917-1958.* NASA SP-4305, 1987.

Dawson, Virginia P. *Engines and Innovation: Lewis Laboratory and American Propulsion Technology.* NASA SP-4306, 1991.

Dethloff, Henry C. *"Suddenly Tomorrow Came . . .": A History of the Johnson Space Center, 1957-1990.* NASA SP-4307, 1993.

Hansen, James R. *Spaceflight Revolution: NASA Langley Research Center from Sputnik to Apollo.* NASA SP-4308, 1995.

Wallace, Lane E. *Flights of Discovery: An Illustrated History of the Dryden Flight Research Center.* NASA SP-4309, 1996.

Herring, Mack R. *Way Station to Space: A History of the John C. Stennis Space Center.* NASA SP-4310, 1997.

Wallace, Harold D., Jr. *Wallops Station and the Creation of an American Space Program.* NASA SP-4311, 1997.

Wallace, Lane E. *Dreams, Hopes, Realities. NASA's Goddard Space Flight Center: The First Forty Years.* NASA SP-4312, 1999.

Dunar, Andrew J. and Waring, Stephen P. *Power to Explore: A History of Marshall Space Flight Center, 1960-1990* NASA SP-4313, 1999.

Bugos, Glenn E. *Atmosphere of Freedom: Sixty years at the NASA Ames Research Center* NASA SP-2000-4314, 2000.

General Histories, NASA SP-4400

Corliss, William R. *NASA Sounding Rockets, 1958-1968: A Historical Summary.* NASA SP-4401, 1971.

Wells, Helen T., Susan H. Whiteley, and Carrie Karegeannes. *Origins of NASA Names.* NASA SP-4402, 1976.

Anderson, Frank W., Jr. *Orders of Magnitude: A History of NACA and NASA, 1915-1980.* NASA SP-4403, 1981.

Sloop, John L. *Liquid Hydrogen as a Propulsion Fuel, 1945-1959.* NASA SP-4404, 1978.

Roland, Alex. *A Spacefaring People: Perspectives on Early Spaceflight*. NASA SP-4405, 1985.

Bilstein, Roger E. *Orders of Magnitude: A History of the NACA and NASA, 1915-1990*. NASA SP-4406, 1989.

Logsdon, John M., ed., with Linda J. Lear, Jannelle Warren Findley, Ray A. Williamson, and Dwayne A. Day. *Exploring the Unknown: Selected Documents in the History of the U.S. Civil Space Program, Volume I, Organizing for Exploration*. NASA SP-4407, 1995.

Logsdon, John M., ed, with Dwayne A. Day, and Roger D. Launius. *Exploring the Unknown: Selected Documents in the History of the U.S. Civil Space Program, Volume II, External Relationships*. NASA SP-4407, 1996.

Logsdon, John M., ed., with Roger D. Launius, David H. Onkst, and Stephen J. Garber. *Exploring the Unknown: Selected Documents in the History of the U.S. Civil Space Program, Volume III, Using Space*. NASA SP-4407,1998.

Logsdon, John M., ed., with Ray A. Williamson, Roger D. Launius, Russell J. Acker, Stephen J. Garber, and Jonathan L. Friedman. *Exploring the Unknown: Selected Documents in the History of the U.S. Civil Space Program, Volume IV, Accessing Space*. NASA SP-4407, 1999.

Logsdon, John M., ed., with Amy Paige Snyder, Roger D. Launius, Stephen J. Garber, and Regan Anne Newport. *Exploring the Unknown: Selected Documents in the History of the U.S. Civil Space Program, Volume V, Exploring the Cosmos*. NASA SP-4407, 2001.

Siddiqi, Asif A., *Challenge to Apollo: The Soviet Union and the Space Race, 1945-1974*. NASA SP-2000-4408.

www.ingramcontent.com/pod-product-compliance
Lightning Source LLC
Chambersburg PA
CBHW080514110426
42742CB00017B/3113